The Diamonds of American Cities

Yale School of Architecture
The Edward P. Bass
Distinguished Visiting
Architecture Fellowship

The Diamonds of American Cities

Janet Marie Smith,
Alan Plattus,
and Andrei Harwell

Published by:
Yale School of Architecture
180 York Street
New Haven, Connecticut 06511
www.architecture.yale.edu

Distributed by:
Actar D
355 Lexington Avenue,
Eighth Floor
New York, NY 10017
www.actar-d.com

This book was made possible through
the Edward P. Bass Distinguished
Visiting Architecture Fellowship fund
of the Yale School of Architecture.
Published through the dean's office,
it is the thirteenth book in the Bass
Fellowship's series.

Editors:
Publications Director:
Nina Rappaport
Assistant Editor: Ron Ostezan
Copy Editor: David Delp

Design: MGMT. design

ISBN: 978-1-9487653-4-3

Edward P. Bass Distinguished Visiting Architecture Fellowship

In 2003 Edward P. Bass, a 1967 graduate of Yale College who studied at the Yale School of Architecture as a member of the class of 1972, endowed this fellowship to bring property developers to the school to lead advanced studios in collaboration with design faculty. An environmentalist and developer, Bass sponsored the Biosphere 2 development in Oracle, Arizona, in 1991, and is responsible for the ongoing revitalization of downtown Fort Worth, Texas, where his Sundance Square, which combines restoration with new construction, has transformed a moribund urban core into a vibrant regional center. In all of his work Bass has been guided by the conviction that architecture is a socially engaged art operating at the intersection of grand visions and everyday realities.

The Bass Fellowship ensures that the school curriculum recognizes the role of the property developer as an integral part of the design process. The program brings developers to Yale to work alongside educators and architecture students in the studio and situate the discussion about architecture in the wider discourse of contemporary practice. The first Bass Studio, led by Gerald Hines and Louis I. Kahn Visiting Professor Stefan Behnisch in 2005, was documented in *Poetry, Property, and Place* (2006). The following year Stuart Lipton, Saarinen Visiting Professor Sir Richard Rogers ('62), engineer Chris Wise, and architect Malcolm Smith (MArch '97) teamed up for the second Bass Studio, documented in *Future-Proofing* (2007). *The Human City* (2008) records the Yale studio collaboration between Roger Madelin and Bishop Visiting Professor Demetri Porphyrios. *Urban Integration: Bishopsgate Goods Yard* (2009) documents the studio led by Nick Johnson and the FAT architecture partnership;

in 2010 Charles Atwood and architect David M. Schwarz's (MArch '74) studio project was published in *Learning in Las Vegas.* The book *Urban Intersections: Sao Paulo* (2011) resulted from the studio led by real estate developer Katherine Farley and architect Deborah Berke. Hong Kong developer Vincent Lo joined Saarinen Visiting Professors Paul Katz, Jamie von Klemperer, and Forth Bagley (BA '99, MArch '01) for the studio described in the book *Rethinking Chongquing: Mixed Use and Super Dense* (2014). Next, *Social Infrastructure: New York* (2015) features the studio led by real estate developer Douglas Durst and Bjarke Ingles of BIG. Furthering the series, Dutch developer Isaac Kalisvaart and Yale's Alexander Garvin (BA '62, MArch '67) and Kevin Gray describe their studio in *The Marine Establissement* (2016). *A Sustainable Bodega and Hotel* (2017) brought together resort property developer John Spence, of the Karma Royal Group, and Saarinen Visiting professors Patrick Bellew, of Atelier Ten, and Andy Bow, of Foster + Partners. *Paranoazinho: City-Making Beyond Brasilia* (2017) presents the analysis and studio led by real estate developers, Rafael Birmann and Ricardo Birmann, of São Paulo, and associate professor (adjunct) Sunil Bald. The studio research and projects led by real estate developer Jonathan Rose with Louis I. Kahn Visiting Assistant Professors Sara Caples (MArch '74) and Everardo Jefferson (MArch '75) was published in *Harlem: Mart 125* (2018). The exhibition and catalog of the Michael Samuelian and Simon Hartmann Bass studio with Andrei Harwell (MArch '06) was featured in *...And More* in May 2019. It is with enthusiasm that we present the in depth work on baseball stadiums led by Janet Marie Smith, senior vice president for planning and development for the Los Angeles Dodgers with Yale faculty Alan Plattus (BA '76) and Andrei Harwell.

Preface
—Deborah Berke, Dean

Janet Marie Smith, the Edward P. Bass Distinguished Visiting Architecture Fellow, is the senior vice president for planning and development for the Los Angeles Dodgers. Before working in sports, Smith was engaged in urban development projects, including Pershing Square in Los Angeles and Battery Park City in New York City, where she served as coordinator of architecture and design under BPC's vice president of planning, Amanda Burden.

Smith holds a bachelor of architecture from Mississippi State University and a master's degree in urban planning from the City University of New York. A former member of engineering firm Syska & Hennessy's board of directors, she is currently an associate member of the Urban Land Institute, the American Institute of Architects, and the American Planning Association and serves on the advisory boards of the Berklee College of Music and the University of Michigan Sports Management Program. Smith has received a fascinatingly broad range of awards and recognitions, from sports writers' associations and women-in-sports business organizations to mayors' councils.

Smith has held several senior Major League Baseball planning and development positions, but she is probably best known for her project for the influential Oriole Park in Baltimore's Camden Yards. She worked for the Orioles as vice president of planning and development during the design and construction of the park, which opened in 1992. She played an instrumental role in the design, creating a facility in an urban context that truly changed that city's downtown and subsequently influenced the redevelopment concepts of many other urban ballparks, an impact that continues to this day.

From 1994 to 2000, she was president of Turner Sports and Entertainment and vice president of planning and development for the Atlanta Braves. Her current position has reunited her with Dodgers' President Stan Kasten; in 1999, they created the Atlanta Hawks' Philips Arena and, in 1997, transformed the 1996 Olympic Stadium into Turner Field.

Smith completed groundbreaking work for Larry Lucchino on the ingenious and sensitive renovation of the Red Sox's Fenway Park, incorporating urban amenities within the sports facility. In fact, *The Boston Globe* has described her as "the architect credited with saving Fenway Park." She also worked on the redevelopment of McCoy Park, home of the Pawtucket Red Sox and the site of the longest baseball game on record (thirty-three innings). Despite her Southern roots, Smith's knowledge of New England baseball is extensive and played a significant role in the Yale students' projects.

As fellow students at City College in urban planning many many years ago I saw Janet's ability to embrace cities as places for all people. Her work as a "developer," a bit broader in terms of what has been the theme of this studio series, looks to sports as public-private partnerships with cities. It could be said that these types of projects have as much impact or even more than large-scale urban downtown revitalization projects. They bring joy as well as opportunity.

As the students will attest, Janet Marie Smith is joyful herself. She is enthusiastic about architecture, design, baseball, and cities—not necessarily in that order. She's also inexhaustible, with boundless energy for the next desk crit or the next enthusiastic cheer at the stadium. Collaborating with the students and faculty of Yale, she shared her expertise for a fruitful and invigorating studio project.

Introduction
—Nina Rappaport and Ron Ostezan

The Diamonds of American Cities presents the design work of MArch students of the thirteenth Edward P. Bass Distinguished Visiting Architecture Fellowship studio, taught at the Yale School of Architecture. Bass Fellow Janet Marie Smith, senior vice president of planning and development for the Los Angeles Dodgers, and Alan Plattus and Andrei Harwell, both Yale School of Architecture faculty members, co-taught the studio in fall 2017.

The studio investigated the role baseball parks can play within their host cities and neighborhoods. At both the major-league and minor-league levels, ballparks present cities with opportunities and challenges in terms of infrastructure and adjacent development as well as entertainment, culture, and tourism. The projects, conversations, and essays presented in this book record a semester of study and analysis of large sports facilities, with a specific focus on contextual approaches to baseball venues and their surrounding urban fabric.

The book starts with an interview with Janet Marie Smith and an essay by Alan Plattus; the latter highlights the studio's conceptual underpinnings—that is, the spatial, social, and economic impact of baseball parks in different urban contexts—and how architecture can contribute to the stewardship of the public realm.

The next section describes the studio's brief, which provided a set of goals and clear objectives that focused students on real-world issues. The class began with Janet Marie Smith's public lecture on the history and future of baseball facilities and their cities, followed by a visit to the studio's first project site in Pawtucket, Rhode Island. Preparatory assignments, research of precedents, site analysis, and visits to baseball games in Boston and Pawtucket introduced students to both the practice and culture of the game and to the opportunities presented by baseball parks as urban anchors. A weeklong study trip to top major- and minor-league ballparks across the country, broadened students' understanding of the way urban ballparks operate and connect with their urban context. From the stands, the class got to watch the Dodgers defeat the San Diego Padres, catapulting the Dodgers into the 2017 post-season.

The next section of the book details the students' studio projects. For the semester's first half, students designed concepts for a new or renovated minor-league park for the Pawtucket Red Sox. Students imagined new relationships within the surrounding context and considered issues at a variety of scales, from seating orientation to future development of adjacent properties. With four different sites in Rhode Island and Massachusetts, each two- or three-student project team developed its own objectives, resulting in a range of approaches and ballpark architecture.

In the second half of the semester, students proposed designs to renovate and expand historic Dodger Stadium and its centerfield area. Applying strategies developed in the first half of the term, they devised schemes to address the future of the fan experience at a Major League Baseball park. Projects explored ways to design a site sandwiched between the modern stadium, designed by Emil Praeger in the late 1950s, and the surrounding surface parking lots.

The book concludes with an interview with Larry Lucchino, president emeritus of the Boston Red Sox and current chairman for the Pawtucket Red Sox, and Stan Kasten, president and CEO of the

Los Angeles Dodgers. The conversation expands upon ideas and themes that students researched throughout the semester as they designed two projects.

The editors would like to recognize the extraordinary effort of the students (all class of 2018) who took part in the studio: Heewon Choi, Daniel Fetcho, Valeria Flores, Zachary Hoffmann, Justin Lai, Audrey Yifei Li, Jiajian Min, Ron Ostezan, Christine Tran, and Dylan Weiser. A special thanks to Emily Walthouse of the Los Angeles Dodgers, planning department for organizing a terrific travel week. We also extend our thanks to our copy editor David Delp, as well as our graphic designers, Sarah Gephart and Minkyoung Kim of MGMT. design.

Pregame Show

A Conversation with Janet Marie Smith

Nina Rappaport You started as an architect and urban planner. How did you become involved in baseball-stadium planning as part of urban redevelopment?

Janet Marie Smith What sparked my interest is my love for cities! I knew very early in my career that I did not want to pursue a traditional architecture practice and preferred managing projects on an urban scale. I really loved the work I did right out of school, coordinating the development of Battery Park City in Manhattan, which meant influencing the shape of the whole cityscape, not just individual buildings. I felt that, by the time the municipality had placed building restrictions on land, the developers had shaped it with programs, and the financial institutions had their bite of the pie, architects didn't have nearly as much voice in how the project was put together, as one might have assumed. I was interested in finding a way to insert myself earlier in the process. In December 1988, after the new Baltimore Orioles ballpark project had been announced, I approached the team because I was intrigued with the idea of building a baseball park in the middle of a city in a way that would redefine downtown. When I was getting my planning degree at City College, I learned about Baltimore's early commitment to revitalization, and I thought, *Wow, here's another way to bring three million people into downtown*!

NR How would you define your role? Would you call yourself a developer?

JMS I think "developer" is a fair term, though not in the way you might imagine, since my approach and work history do not fit neatly into a category. I am often frustrated that architects are not inserted early in the dialogue of city-building and aren't brought into the discussion until the program is set. Our education teaches us to think broadly, yet we are often in the position of giving shape to a program that has had no input from an architect. Similarly, a developer doesn't always get to define how their projects, whether housing, office buildings, or retail, are pulled together. There are many ways of shaping a city using the tools of a developer, pulling together constituencies, working to select a site and construct a budget, selecting tenants, graphics, photo moments, and the sort of animation that creates a memorable place in the city with uses and amenities. I've loved being in a position where I can put together a design team that can make those things happen.

NR For such a long time people felt that stadiums needed space around them for parking and access, so how did the Baltimore ballpark project become a new paradigm for stadiums returning to and revitalizing the heart of a city?

JMS Several things happened at once. First, the multipurpose-stadium era ended. It had survived from the 1960s into the '80s and was used as a tool for clearing hundreds of acres of land, just as the "tower in the plaza" and big-box architecture were products of the same period. However, this approach didn't work in terms of the mix of uses and the level of vitality. These projects were very expensive because they had to be built at once, and the infrastructure costs were enormous. These projects could not be financed. A more "contextual" approach became the new model of integrating stadiums into

the urban center. The approach used existing parking, mass transit, and roadways, and it was a less expensive investment. And like other urban planning and architectural trends, the big box was out and context was in. Specifically, for Baltimore, William Donald Schaefer, the state governor and a former mayor of the city, was committed to this urban location, and the Orioles team president and CEO at the time, Larry Lucchino, was inspired to build a baseball-only park with old-fashioned charm and modern amenities. These two guiding principles were in distinct support of each other.

NR What have been some of the biggest challenges for you in these urban redevelopment projects in terms of infrastructure?

JMS This is always a big issue, as transit and parking and traffic patterns are in any new development, and my current work at

View of Oriole Park at Camden Yards from left field.

Dodgers Stadium in Los Angeles is a perfect example. Opened in 1962, it is now the third-oldest baseball park. Architecturally significant because of its unique design, carved into the hillside of Chavez Ravine, it was constructed at a time when the Dodgers were focused solely on bringing their 56,000 fans to the park via automobiles. There was no mass transit, nor had there been any serious discussion about bringing it to the site to create regional connections. As Los Angeles has changed and people have become more reliant on mass transit, it has transformed the way people move around. So, the challenge has been to rethink access–how people use their cars today and alternate transportation, from mass transit to ride share to trends to live near work. As the city of Los Angeles grows around this beautiful hilltop park, we want to get ahead of the transportation curve, and that is a regional problem we need to address.

Entry to Dodger Stadium on the Reserve Level.

NR Historic preservation also has a role in your work, such as in Baltimore, where you saved the historic B&O warehouse building and made it part of the ballpark, and in Boston, where you helped rescue Fenway Park, guiding the Red Sox to develop a strategy to renovate the oldest park in the major league. How has the history of these ballparks been a part of your approach for building preservation?

JMS Besides the respect for history, it is the realization that buildings don't have to have extraordinary traditional architectural character to be extraordinary buildings. There is something magical about the warehouse's link to Baltimore's past, for example. Twenty-eight years ago, during the planning stages, Lucchino really wanted the new baseball park to have an asymmetrical playing field, the kind of quirkiness you saw in older parks, such as Ebbets Field in Brooklyn, Forbes Field in Pittsburgh, Shibe Park in Philadelphia, or Fenway Park in Boston. This asymmetry came about authentically because of the constraints of the urban environment. Our disposable society is quick to say, "Let's tear it down and start over." The environmentally responsible thing to do is to reuse what we have and not be so whimsical about bricks and mortar. The warehouse at Camden Yards was preserved for a variety of reasons, but, for one thing, it ensured the authenticity of the project and allowed us to avoid giving it a Disney-like quality.

NR Another urban issue is how downtown sports venues haven't used their assets well enough in terms of multiple uses for consumers. How have projects such as Fenway Park, whose design incorporates adjacent buildings, become part of the commercial life of neighborhoods?

JMS One thing we've tried to do—and maybe this is how I get cast in the role of a developer in the Yale nomenclature—is to think through not just what buildings will look like and how we will use the spaces but also how we can influence the business strategies that will give buildings life. That's the key to everything. What is housed in that architecture is really the reason for the success of the ballpark as an urban building. At both Oriole Park at Camden Yards and Fenway Park in Boston, we tried to place everything that could have a life beyond the baseball game—the team store, the ticket office, the food and beverage concessions, team memorabilia—where it could enliven the street and have an urban presence and be open every day. Certainly, there's an economic incentive for the team to run a year-round operation, but a game-day-only operation is not responsible urban development. As teams have felt compelled to add more premium areas to their parks, they are creating more enclosed space and functioning as media and convention centers with an appropriate mix of uses. It is no accident that many cities, including Baltimore, have found a synergy in building adjacent convention centers.

NR What makes a great ballpark?

JMS I gravitate toward the way people use urban space. To me, a ballpark's success is measured by how seamlessly people move from the core urban environment into these buildings and out again, having their tickets scanned and taking in nine innings of baseball as part of an urban experience. That is what makes spectator sports special: stadiums are one of the few places in American society where people of different backgrounds and socioeconomic means come together, cheering for the same thing. In a way, they are like public parks, though there is an admission price! They function as a civic space, and in all my projects we've tried to think about how we can be responsible for the civic role sports play in our society and how we can create a place where everyone feels ownership. The ballpark belongs to three million people every year; we are just stewards of that for the time we are there.

NR Which ballpark has brought you both the biggest challenges and the most satisfaction?

JMS Oriole Park at Camden Yards, my first involvement in the sports arena, was wonderful, and as it turned out, it wasn't just a flash in the pan. It changed the trajectory of thinking about sports venues and their roles in cities. Fenway Park was special because, for more than twenty years, the Red Sox presumed that they were going to have to leave the ballpark for a venue that met the new programmatic requirements of what the major leagues demanded in order to remain competitive. It was like pulling it from the brink of a raging river to be able to find a way to do renovations and additions within the economic constraints of the team's funding. We took buildings that the Red Sox owned and used for other purposes and attached them functionally to Fenway Park. We worked within the National Park Service's historic guidelines to make certain those buildings were treated in a way that was respectful of their architecture and their role in the history of the Back Bay neighborhood. Dodger Stadium is totally different: It's a 1960s building designed of patterned concrete block with corrugated metal, and it is carved into the hillside and has a crazy inverted precast roof. Because of its scale and relationship to nearby Elysian Park, the landscape is as much a defining feature as the brick and mortar. It has been an enormous thrill to reimagine that baseball stadium—with arguably the best sight lines in all of baseball but very few fan amenities—trying to find a way to create these social spaces inside while changing its image from a park in a parking lot to a park in a park. It has also given me a chance to work with landscape architects in a more intense way than I've had the opportunity to do in other settings.

NR In Europe, there are more experimental designs for stadiums. Why are there so few similar innovations in the United States?

JMS Many of the recent stadiums in the United States were considered innovations for their time in a different way: rather than look-at-me buildings, baseball has trended toward the way a park can be a part of the urban tapestry. As more and more teams have moved into cities, architects have incorporated hometown characteristics into the park as an urban context: Cleveland's structure recalls its bridges, and San Diego has outdoor porches that resonate with the convention center and the water views behind the ballpark.

* This conversation was published in *Constructs* Spring 2018.

top View towards the outfield of Dodger Stadium.

bottom View of Fenway Park from above.

top View towards the outfield bleachers and Elysian Park from Dodger Stadium's Top Deck.

bottom View of Eutaw Street within Oriole Park at Camden Yards.

Minor League, Back to the Majors —Alan Plattus

There is no doubt that the iconic monuments of the sport of baseball are the thirty current major-league ballparks in the United States and Canada, though many of their now vanished predecessors have the advantage of living only in our memory, in terms of representational power. These structures have often–to the point of cliché–been compared to medieval cathedrals, and not only as sites of secular mass religion but also for the role that they play as *Stadtkrone* ("city crowns") –in their respective host cities. But the urban spatial culture of baseball is far more widely disseminated in cities and towns across North America and around the world by the countless local ballparks–parish churches, perhaps–of American Legion teams, international Little League, and the more than three hundred professional minor-league teams, affiliated or unaffiliated with parent Major League Baseball clubs. While many of the major-league ballparks have passed into the realm of self-reference, having become images or, like the "new" Yankee Stadium–copies of themselves, not to mention the increasing financial alienation of the game and its players vis-à-vis the daily lives of most ordinary urban residents, the minor-league game and its ballparks have been (and for the most part, have been compelled to be) leaders and innovators in civic and spatial engagement within their urban settings.

Baseball has been a quintessentially local, if not always suburban, game from its quasi-mythic beginnings on the Elysian Fields in Hoboken, New Jersey, in 1845. Early ballparks were neighborhood institutions, and until the major shift in scale and construction type that mostly developed in the early twentieth century, did not radically interrupt the fabric of the city block into which they fit more or less naturally. In that regard, early major-league ballparks were quite similar to the latest generation of minor-league parks, of which more in a moment. Even the big new urban ballparks of the early twentieth century–Shibe Park in Philadelphia, Ebbets Field in Brooklyn, Fenway Park in Boston, Wrigley Park in Chicago, and the House that Ruth Built, Yankee Stadium in the Bronx–had elaborate façade treatments, masking their new steel structures and bulk, mediating and normalizing the relationship with the surrounding city streets, and heightening the sense of liminal passage from the street to the magical realm of the field inside.

In the post-war era, with teams moving west, new franchises, and urban renewal-based replacements of older ballparks, instigated a generation of concrete "spaceships" more or less oblivious to their often bulldozed urban context, instead mimicking each other, and worst of all, trying to be "multipurpose," for baseball and football and serving neither particularly well. One thinks of Three Rivers Stadium replacing Forbes Field in Pittsburgh, Riverfront replacing Crosley Field in Cincinnati, the new Astrodome in Houston, and others. Not only were these new facilities opaque and placeless, they were an order of magnitude bigger than the ballparks they replaced, alienating not only baseball from

the surrounding city but also the many fans from the intimacy and intricacy of the action in the field of play.

The counterrevolution in terms of a re-engagement with local place, history, and architecture, as well as with the traditions of the game, and with an appreciation of scale and variety in shaping "fan experience," began in Baltimore with Camden Yards. This concept spread rapidly not only with new construction affecting not only new construction but also with sympathetic renovations of surviving historic ballparks. Now familiar, these design strategies—such as incorporating a site's existing historic structures, celebrating the pressures and idiosyncrasies of the urban context, and opening the ballpark to views of the city, as "borrowed" views or as a backdrop to the spectacle on the field—were tropes that could be reproduced and adapted to local circumstances,

Students touring Regions Field in Birmingham.

making each ballpark seem to be a unique experience and a product of its particular place. Design firms (HOK Sports, for example), executives (Larry Lucchino, the Red Sox CEO and president), and consultants (Janet Marie Smith) soon adopted this mission as their own. Similar design trends trickled down to influence new minor-league construction in places such as Memphis, which had major-league ambitions, and fostered local pride in historic minor-league ballparks, far more of which had survived the building boom of the Sixties and could now inspire affection and nostalgia rather than simply seeming tired, rundown, and provincial.

Indeed, to be visibly provincial was no longer seen as pejorative but positively fashionable and, therefore, marketable. In that regard, the irreducibly local character, small-scale intimacy, and accessibility of older minor-league parks were the "real thing" that state-of-the-art new major-league ballparks could learn from as much as from vanished icons like Ebbets Field and survivors like Fenway. One lesson was simply size, as major-league ballparks scaled back to 35,000 seats from the 50,000- to 60,000-seat range. Those numbers were still gigantic and corporate compared to the typical minor-league park, where one could often actually see everyone in attendance and easily stroll through the stands and never be far from the field. Many of these older parks retained a quite casual relationship to their surroundings, with a less radical distinction between being "outside" the park versus inside, with a ticket–the least expensive purchase of an afternoon at the ballpark. In Billings, Montana, the local Pioneer League rookie team, the Mustangs, play in Dehler Park, where the field is below street level and more or less open to, and visible from, the surrounding city streets. This sense of porosity and blurring of outside and inside are to be found in new minor-league parks, such as the ambitious new home of the Triple-A Nashville Sounds and the major-league Petco Park in San Diego, although its adjacent public park near left field is actually within the ticketed area on game days.

It is no accident that a the classic baseball movie *Bull Durham*, comically but lovingly depicting the small-town culture and human drama of the minor-leagues–some players and towns on their way up, while others achingly play out their string–would be set in just such a classic minor-league ballpark. Indeed, Durham North Carolina, has lovingly preserved, restored, and continues to use that old stadium, even as it has constructed an impressive new ballpark with character as part of a downtown revitalization program that includes an arts center, the adaptive re-use of the former American Tobacco factory complex, and several new boutique hotels in renovated Art Deco and Modern buildings; further, minor-league baseball has become an integral part of the comprehensive repurposing of a once tired small urban downtown in the new economy of meds and eds, spectacle and consumption. Birmingham, Alabama, has also protected its 1910 Rickwood Stadium, longtime home to both the Birmingham Barons of the Double-A Southern League and the Black Barons of the old Negro National League. The Barons moved to the suburbs in the 1980s but have recently returned to an impressive new ballpark that follows the contextual logic of recent development but with a less-than-literal architectural vocabulary inspired by the industrial traditions of steel-producing Birmingham, rather than the now ubiquitous brick veneer of so many recent major-league facilities.

Ruins of the Sloss Blast Furnaces, Birmingham, which influenced HKS in the design of Regions Field.

In general, minor-league ballparks, as well as their programming, are tending to take more chances and be more quirky and imaginative and more directly engaged with their contexts and communities than their better capitalized, more corporate, and media-driven major-league parents. That is not surprising, given minor-league baseball's financial and market constraints and the fact, as pointed out by Larry Lucchino, that, while most folks who shell out for a once- or twice-a-year pilgrimage to a major-league stadium are there primarily for the baseball and only secondarily there for the beer and hotdogs, minor-league franchises, which do not actually own their players and change personnel with unpredictable frequency, must market the fan experience, including food, silly entertainment between innings, and a variety of ways to "be at the ballpark." Design or renovation of a minor-league facility is likely to include not just skyboxes for high rollers—of which there may be only a few—but also special pavilions, bar-style seating, picnic areas on grassy knolls, and activities for fans of all ages, since, increasingly, baseball is billed as a family-friendly experience. As a result of a new wave of invention, promotion, community outreach, and "local" color, minor-league baseball has not only become as much a successor to the American circus with the continuity between generations of local baseball, it has also (we learned this semester) begun to have a trickle-up effect on the way that Major League Baseball ballparks are designed and renovated. Most of all, the new designs are due to the persistence and renewal at the minor-league level of that sense of intimacy, and even accessibility, that is so distinctive of baseball. For those who treasure this dimension of the game, there is also the speculative anticipation of watching and even perhaps getting to know the future superstars of the major-league club before they retreat to the mediated realm of layers of agents, security, and spectacle, doubly insulated by stratospheric salaries and ticket prices. At the major-league level, that close, casual spatial connection with the game and the players is, for the most part, only available at spring training—when the ballparks continue to be intimate and local. As good as the recent wave of major-league parks in places such as Pittsburgh, San Diego, and San Francisco may be, they seem to be at their best when, like the minor leagues, they really connect to local place and community.

Batter Up
A Studio in Two Parts

Studio Brief

This Bass studio explored urban design, development opportunities and challenges of large sports facilities in their host cities and neighborhoods. In particular, the students considered the spatial, social, and economic impact of baseball stadiums in different urban contexts. Traditionally, professional baseball has been an urban experience and a source of identity in cities and towns across the country and now around the world. However, post–World War II, as American urban development became more suburbanized and automobile-oriented and a number of baseball franchises moved to new locations from older cities, the typology and siting of baseball stadiums changed radically, especially for Major League Baseball. These moves often involved building generic facilities to accommodate not only baseball but also other sports and events. While Dodger Stadium exemplified the shift toward auto-oriented patterns of access, it was an exception to the multipurpose-stadium trend and sited near the city center but woven into a park design rather than the city grid. With the Camden Yards development by the Baltimore Orioles organization from 1989 to 1992, an effort led, in part, by Janet Marie Smith, the development pattern began to change again. Since then, older facilities in historic cities,

opposite View of downtown Los Angeles from Dodger Stadium

like Fenway Park in Boston and Wrigley Field in Chicago, have been restored, renovated, and adapted to modern patterns of use while conserving their image and relationship to the surrounding urban fabric. Emulating the Camden Yards model, precisely for its urban intimacy, character, and even spatial idiosyncrasies, new facilities seek to learn lessons from older ballparks, such as how their designs incorporate the particularities and flavor of their respective urban settings. Not merely a matter of architectural character or style, the new designs have involved a careful study of scale, mixture of uses,

patterns of circulation, and the rituals and experience of baseball itself. The impact of these developments has reached far beyond the major urban centers that have Major League Baseball teams, affecting medium-size cities and even small towns with minor-league and independent teams, as well as throughout the spring-training venues of the Grapefruit League in Florida and the Cactus League in Arizona.

Students studied a range of scales, sites, and circumstances through visits to baseball parks across the country, the development of detailed analytic studies of a variety of stadiums, and the design of two quite different projects that two well-established organizations are currently considering. The first project design, completed at midterm, involved the design of a new or redeveloped facility in Rhode Island or Massachusetts for the Pawtucket Red Sox, or PawSox, the AAA farm team of the Boston Red Sox. Here, students were challenged to use minor-league ballparks as a design template to create a catalyst for urban development and an identity for an underdeveloped, post-industrial New England mill town. After midterm, the studio focused on a very different project: the redevelopment of Dodger Stadium at Chavez Ravine in Los Angeles, an icon of postwar Modernism and urban renewal (the Dodgers

opposite top **The view from the upper concourse of Regions Field.**

opposite bottom **View of the entrance to AutoZone Park in Memphis from the rooftop terrace of The Peabody building.**

REGIONS FIELD

top Students touring McCoy Stadium.

bottom Students on the field pregame at Fenway Park.

moved there in 1962 after leaving Ebbets Field in Brooklyn in 1958). The students were asked to reinvent Dodger Stadium so that it better integrates with Los Angeles and its neighborhoods. In both cases, the development of successful projects hinged on the ability to work simultaneously at different scales, from large-scale infrastructure and building structures to the interior details and exterior public spaces—all informed by materials, visual relationships, lighting, and landscape.

On trips throughout the term, the students visited Dodger Stadium and other major-league parks on the West Coast, several newer minor-league parks in the South, and McCoy Stadium and other baseball parks on the East Coast. While focused on stadium architecture, the studio considered how a large sports facility can serve not only baseball but also interests beyond baseball, encouraging a catalytic network of spatial and productive relationships within the surrounding city. The studio also considered the game of baseball itself, its spatial, cultural, and political dimensions, as a highly structured experience, as a business and a global brand, and as a source of identity, competition, and even conflict within and among cities.

Precedent Studies for Minor-League Baseball Parks

Compared to their major-league counterparts, minor-league ballparks are more playful in their design and more family-oriented and rooted in local traditions. For example, Regions Field in Birmingham features brick details, large steel spans, and other local architectural elements. Each student analyzed a minor-league ballpark and prepared a series of drawings for comparison, indicating scale, the ballpark's urban site, and its general formal characteristics.

Students studied a minor-league ballpark to familiarize themselves with baseball and to analyze each urban situation.

Comparative Analysis of Minor-League Baseball Stadiums

Urban Location Plan
1 mi. radius @ 1" = 1000'

Context Plan
1/4 mi. radius @ 1" = 250'

Axonometric Drawing
@ 1" = 100'

AutoZone Park
Memphis Redbirds, Memphis, TN
By Valeria Flores

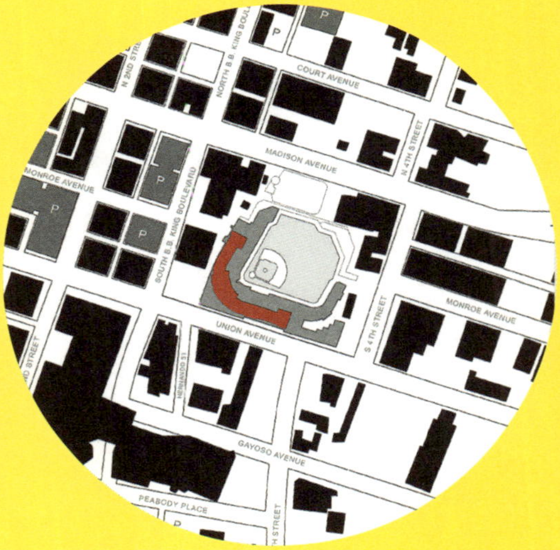

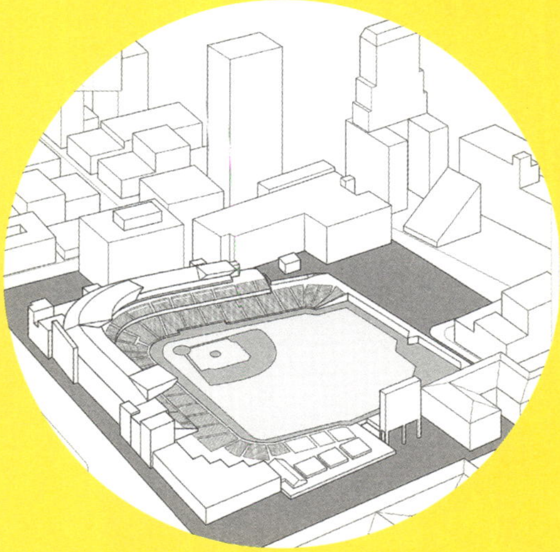

BB&T Ballpark
Charlotte Knights, Charlotte, NC
By Min Jiajian

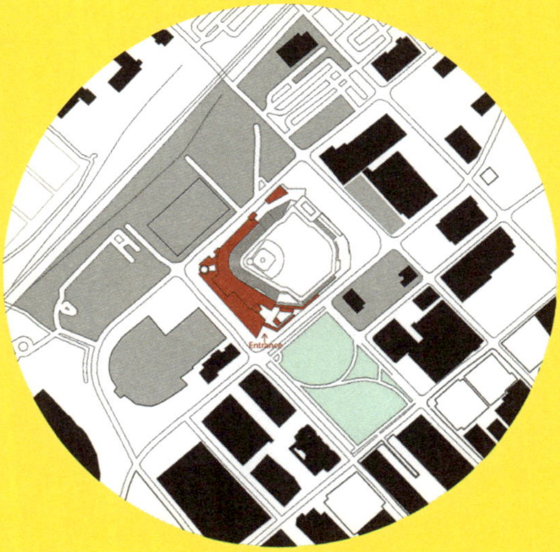

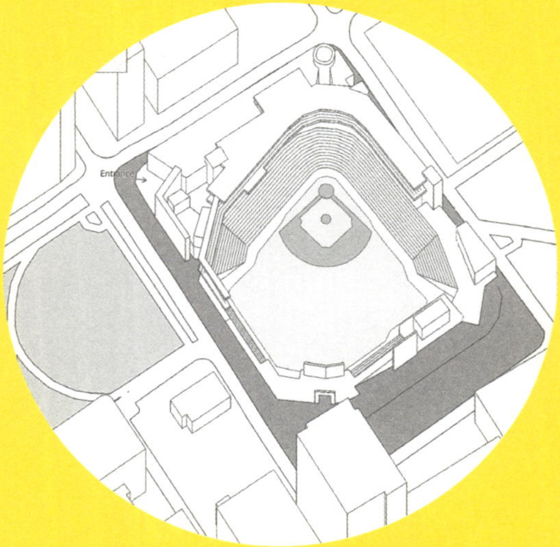

Coca-Cola Park
LeHigh Valley IronPigs, Allentown, PA
By Justin Lai

Dr Pepper Ballpark
Frisco RoughRiders, Frisco, TX
By Daniel Fetcho

Urban Location Plan: 1 mi. radius @ 1" = 1000'

Context Plan: 1/4 mi. radius @ 1" = 250'

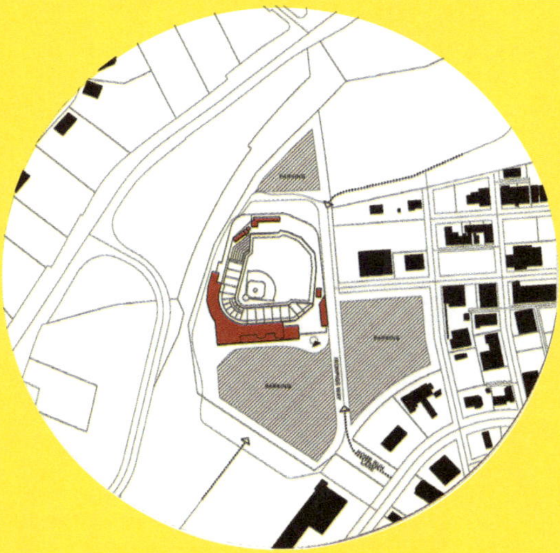

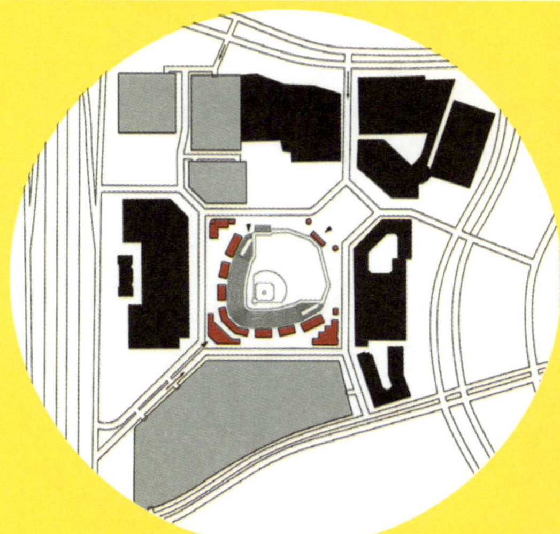

Axonometric Drawing @ 1" = 100'

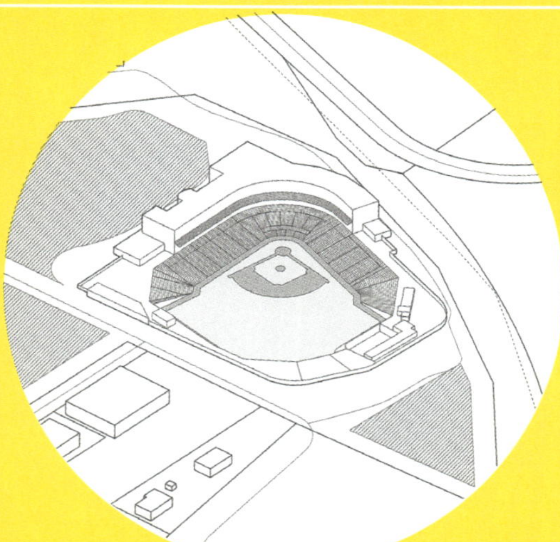

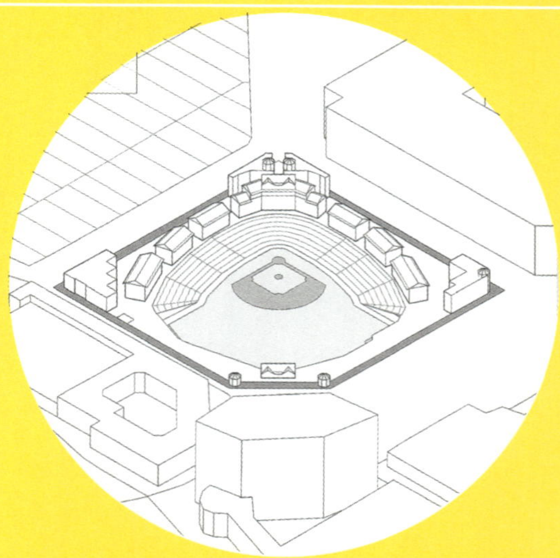

Dunkin Donuts Park
Hartford Yard Goats, Hartford, CT
By Zachary Hoffmann

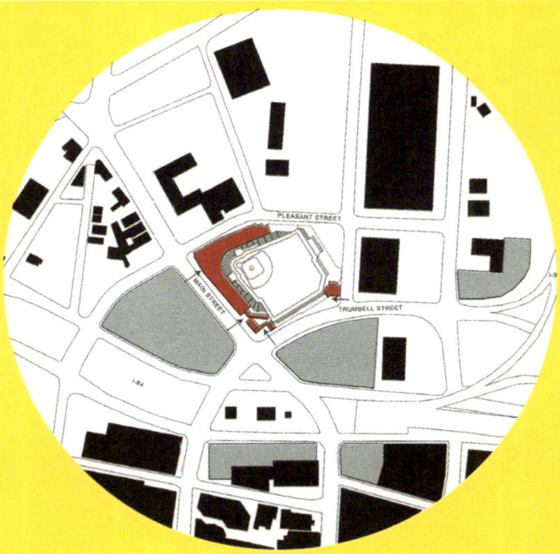

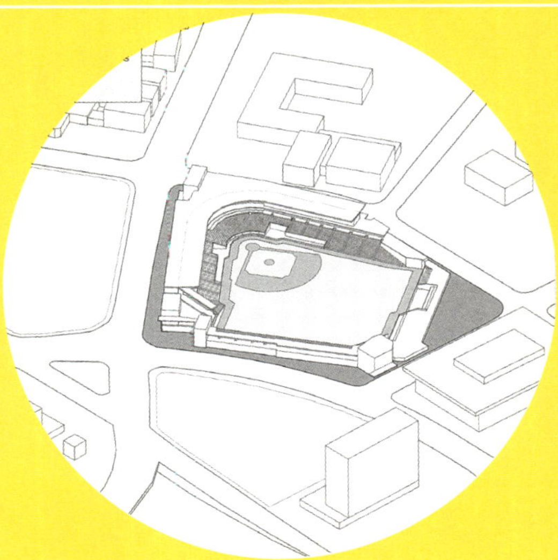

Fifth Third Field
Toledo Mud Hens, Toledo, OH
By Ronald Ostezan

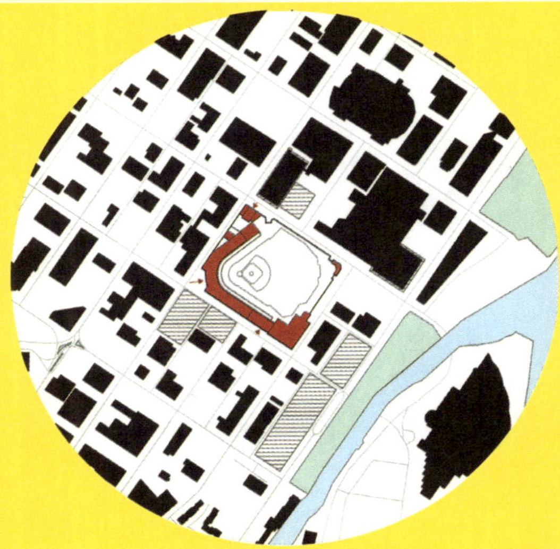

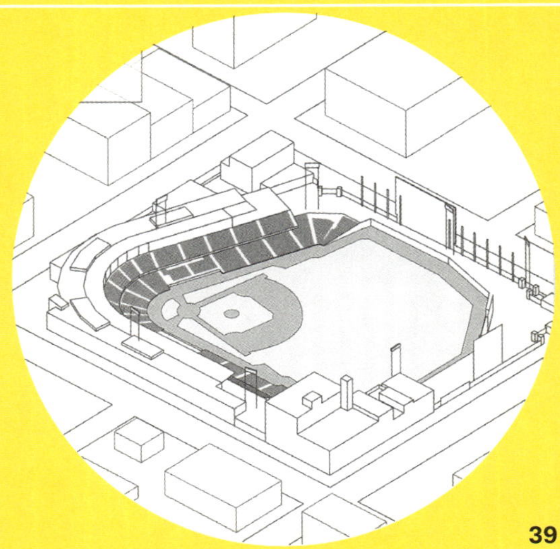

First Tennessee Park
Nashville Sound, Nashville, TN
By Dylan Weiser

Huntington Park
Columbus Clippers, Columbus, OH
By Audrey Yifei Li

Urban Location Plan: 1 mi. radius @ 1" = 1000'

Context Plan: 1/4 mi. radius @ 1" = 250'

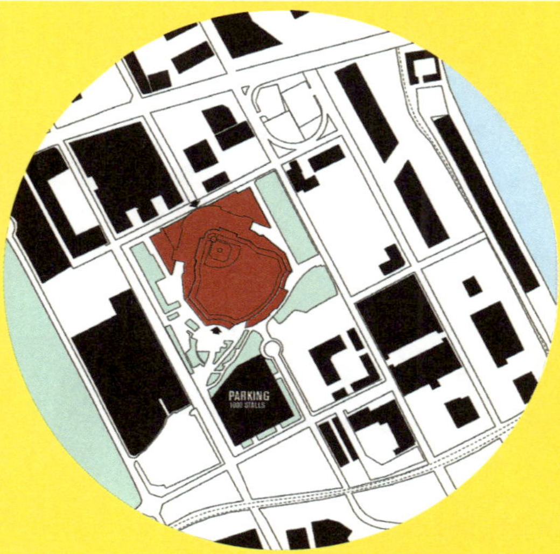

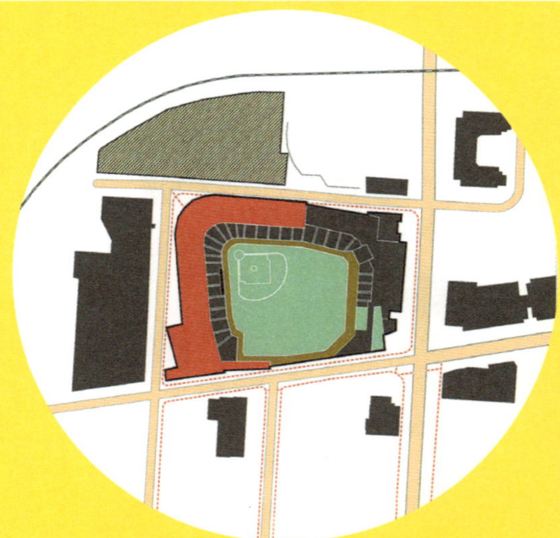

Axonometric Drawing @ 1" = 100'

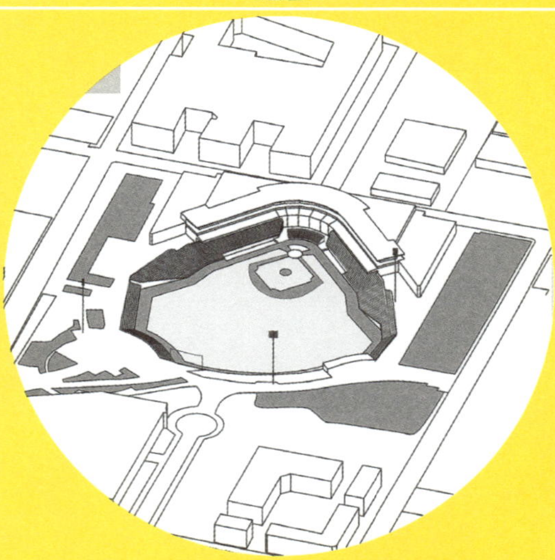

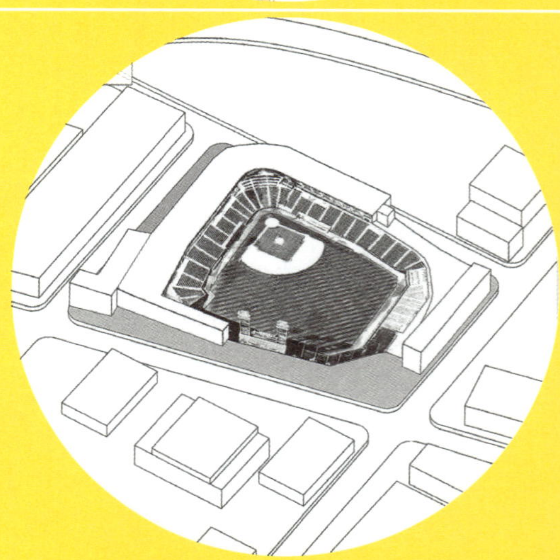

Louisville Slugger Field
Louisville Bats, Louisville, KY
By Heewon Choi

Rickwood Field
Birmingham Barons (formerly), Birmingham, AL
By Christine Tran

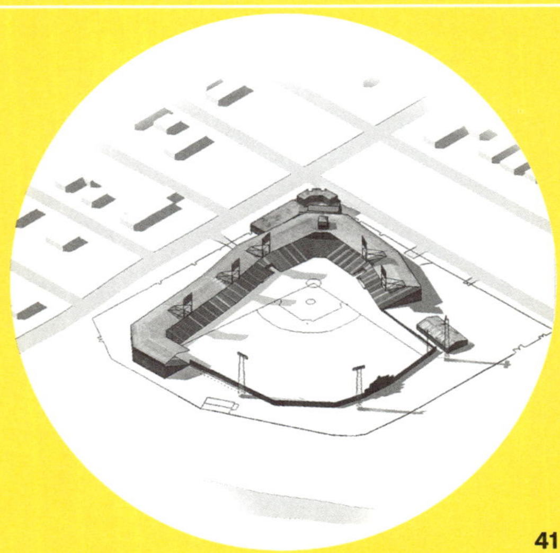

Studio Travel

The semester began with a visit to McCoy Stadium, the Pawtucket, Rhode Island, home of the AAA minor-league Pawtucket Red Sox ball club and one of four sites for the first project of the semester. Students learned about baseball, ballpark requirements, and the relationship between sports facilities and their surroundings. Constructed as a WPA project in the early 1940s, McCoy Stadium is the oldest minor-league ballpark in use today and features a steel-truss canopy that shelters a seating bowl. Three other sites were considered for the ballpark: a redevelopment of an area adjacent to the Seekonk River and the Slater Mill Historic Site, in downtown Pawtucket; a former industrial site and brownfield in Attleboro, Massachusetts; and a brownfield site in the Canal District in downtown Worcester, Massachusetts.

Students also visited Boston's Fenway Park, then met with Tom Martinez (DAIQ Architects), who led the design of the facility's renovation, and Larry Cancro, senior vice president of the Red Sox, to understand the possibilities of ballparks beyond game days and within the fabric of a city.

opposite top **Field-level view of Dodger Stadium from the centerfield warning track.**

opposite middle **Seating-bowl view into the outfield at McCoy Stadium.**

opposite bottom **Students touring Dodger Stadium.**

SCHWAB
A. SCHWAB
A. Schwab

To begin their week of travel, students visited Dodger Stadium, where Dodgers President and CEO Stan Kasten and other Dodger executives provided information on the organization's priorities and goals. The students saw the last home game of the season, which the Dodgers won 10–0 against the San Diego Padres. The following day, the studio was given a comprehensive tour that highlighted Emil Praeger's late-1950s design. The stadium is a symmetrical, rounded triangular form, built into a hill to achieve a 125-foot grade change from one end of the ballpark to the other. The intent of this design was on-grade parking and entry for every seating area. Primarily constructed of concrete and light-blue folded metal, the main seating bowl is covered by a poured-in-place concrete roof, with zigzag metal roofs and now-iconic hexagonal scoreboards sheltering the outfield pavilions. Janet Marie Smith and her team updated the stadium by expanding the entrance plazas, which were sympathetic to the historic structure's aesthetic. Her team developed easier circulation around the ballpark, widening concourses, retrofitting to ADA standards, and establishing larger fan zones. Smith supervised the design of the park's new themed areas, such as around the 76 gas station, bullpen overlooks, history and memorabilia sections, and landscaped zones.

opposite top **View down Beale Street in Memphis.**

opposite bottom **View inside the Western Metal Supply Co. building at Petco Park, a former warehouse.**

In San Diego, students visited Petco Park, a major-league park designed in 2004 by Antoine Predock and HOK Sport. While the sandstone construction and its red hues evoke the Southern California context, the white-painted steel beams mimic sailboats in the bay and two towers rise up like mission bell towers. Concessions and other programs are pulled away from the field to provide views into the park, the downtown area, and the historic Western Metal Supply Co. factory, which is incorporated into left field, a move inspired by the way Camden Yard integrated its own historic context. After a tour through the outfield, concourses, club-level suites, and the Home Plate Club, students saw a game between prospects of the Padres and Texas Rangers.

After the California tour of major-league ballparks, the students drove through Memphis, Birmingham, and Nashville to see minor-league ballparks, noting their intimate scale and how they integrated with local communities. In Memphis, they saw AutoZone Park, home to the minor-league Memphis Redbirds, and heard from Josh Whitehead, director of planning and development for the city of Memphis, who talked about how the ballpark has catalyzed extensive redevelopment. They also met with Ray Brown, James

opposite **An interior view of the Crosstown Concourse, a former Sears warehouse.**

McLaren, and other members of the Downtown Memphis Commission to discuss the financing of the ballpark, the goals of the project, and the development opportunities afforded by its construction. To study historic preservation precedents, students visited the renovated Peabody Hotel, a Bass Pro Shop housed in the converted Pyramid arena, and the Crosstown Concourse, an arts-based

mixed-use development in a former Sears distribution center.

In Birmingham, Alabama, designer Byron Chambers led the students on a tour of Regions Field, where the AA Barons play. After the tour, Bill Mudd and Alison Nichols hosted a traditional Southern lunch for the students at their B&A warehouse. Mudd, labeled as the only "holdout" when the Barons sought to acquire the land for their ballpark, spoke of his experience with the surrounding development. Students also visited Rickwood Field (1910), the oldest minor-league ballpark still standing today, followed by a visit to the Sloss Blast Furnaces (1882) site, which served as inspiration for the design of Regions Field.

Finally, in Nashville, they visited First Tennessee Park, home of the Nashville Sounds, a AAA minor-league ballclub. With Lucy Kempf, manager of land development at the Metro Nashville Planning Department, the studio discussed the impact of the ballpark and saw diverse seating areas and activity zones. Hastings Architecture Associates—the local architect for Populous, the design architect—presented the ballpark development and Nashville's intense growth over the past decade. The trip down South ended with an Opry Country Classics concert.

View toward home plate from down the left field line at Petco Park.

First Pitch Pawtucket Red Sox

The first design project focused on the Pawtucket Red Sox (PawSox). Organized into four teams, the students designed a stadium and adjacent development at four different sites. One team designed the renovation scheme for McCoy Stadium, the PawSox's home. This project was conceived in parallel to the organization's efforts to identify a direction for the team's future home, now known to be a move to Worcester, in 2021.

Since three of the four sites called for a new field, the students considered development opportunities as well as the specifics of their ballparks, with a focus on minor-league-ballpark requirements. Prioritizing the fans' experience of real-time games and speculating on how that experience might change in the future, the students designed inventive activity zones, next-gen seating arrangements, and new public areas of interaction and possibility. In short, the studio did not limit architecture's scope to the stadium itself or the area's existing conditions but allowed it the freedom to create moments of joy and communal experience through place-making. As the PawSox make plans for the stadium in Worcester, the organization took notes on each of the four teams' projects, which were persuasive partly due to their high degree of articulation.

top Seating bowl and canopy at McCoy Stadium.

middle The Attleboro team presenting its project at mid-term reviews.

bottom View of existing concourse at McCoy Stadium, showing its low ceiling height and poor lighting.

Site Research

1.1

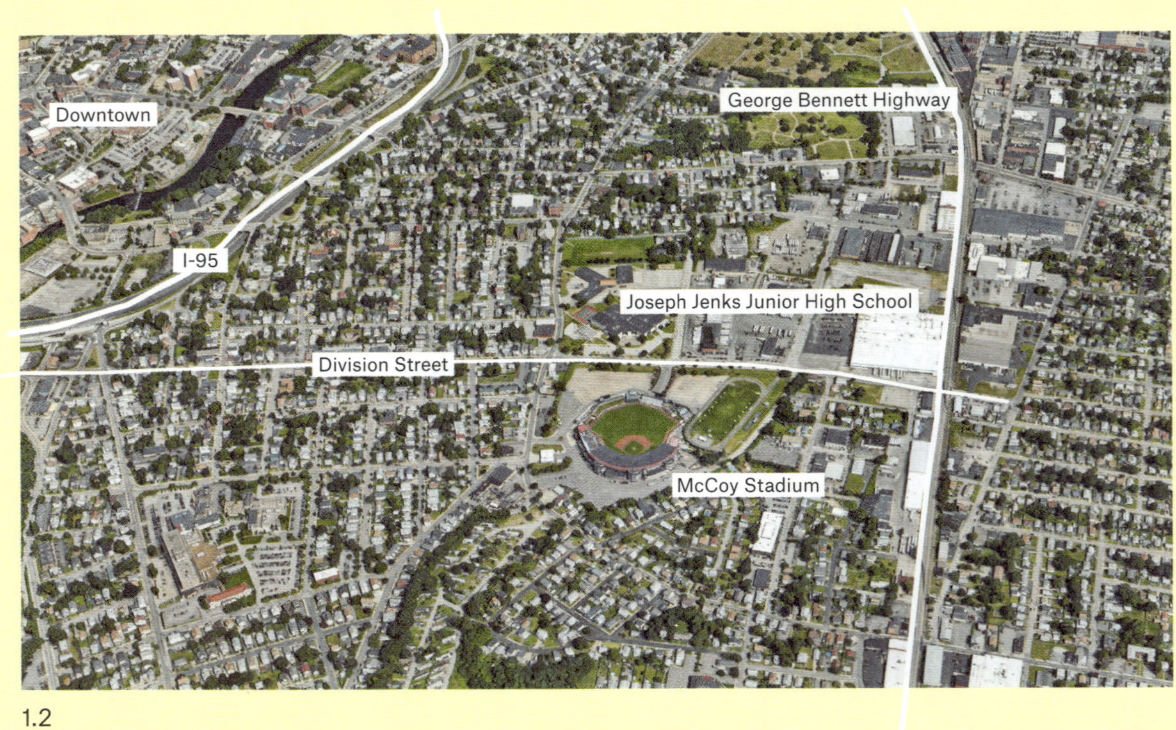

1.2

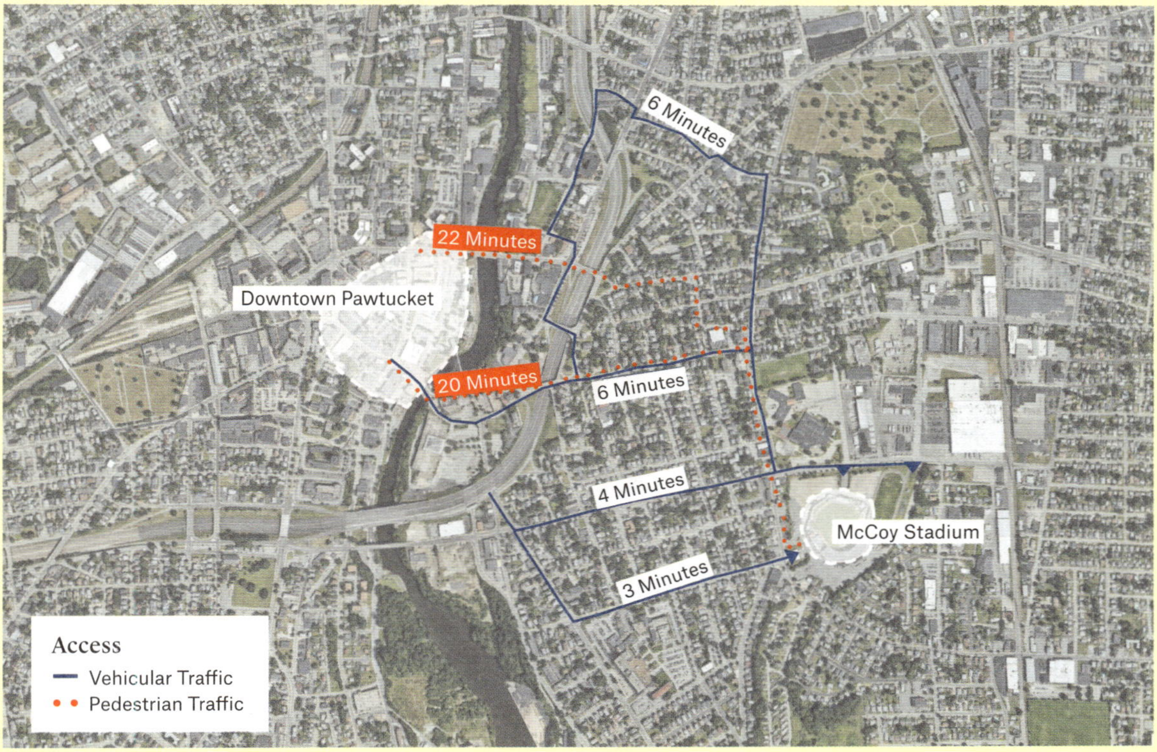

1.3

1.1 Teams of students worked on one of four different sites for the first project. Two were located in Pawtucket, with the other two in Attleboro and Worcester. Pawtucket is forty miles from Worcester and Boston.

1.2 Diagram of McCoy Stadium and its access points.

1.3 Access to McCoy Stadium from downtown Pawtucket or the off-ramp from the highway.

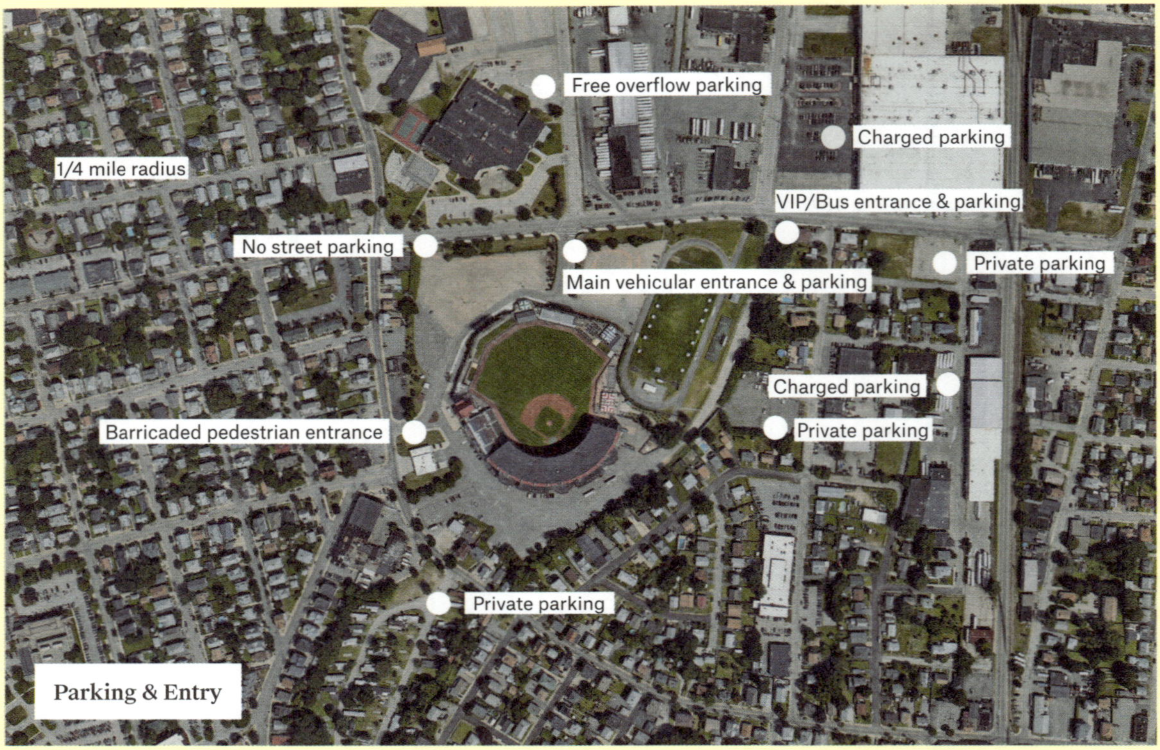

1.4

1.4 Diagram of McCoy Stadium's entrances and the ballpark's parking.

1.5 Existing programming at McCoy Stadium.

McCoy Stadium Existing Conditions

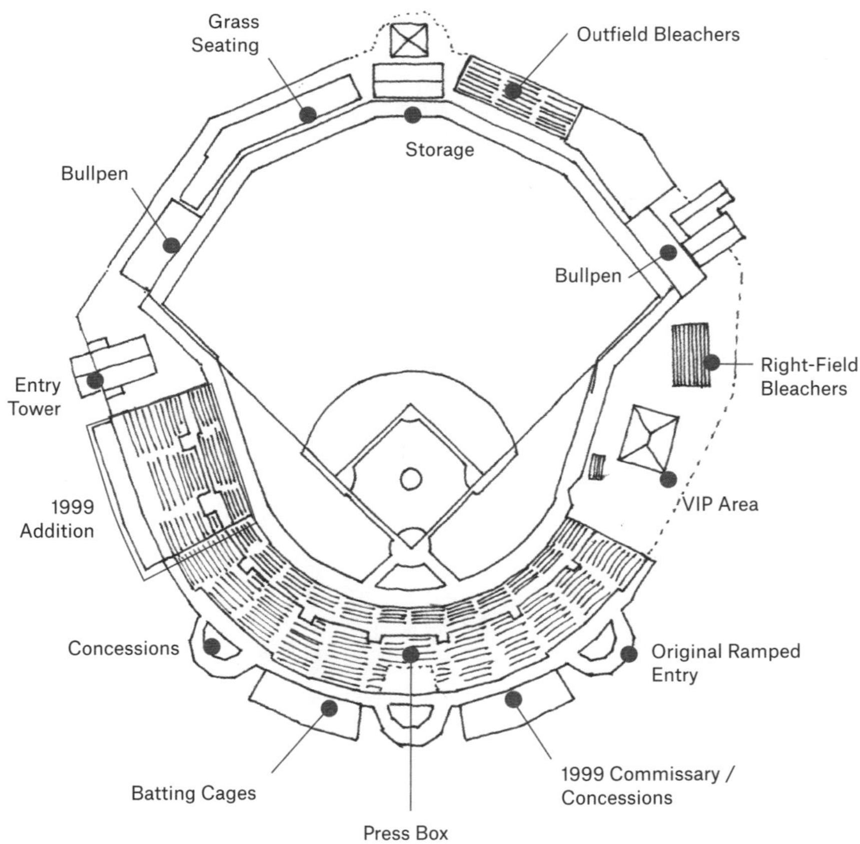

1.5

Railroad
Proposed Commuter Rail station
Downtown
I-95
Site
McCoy Stadium

1.6

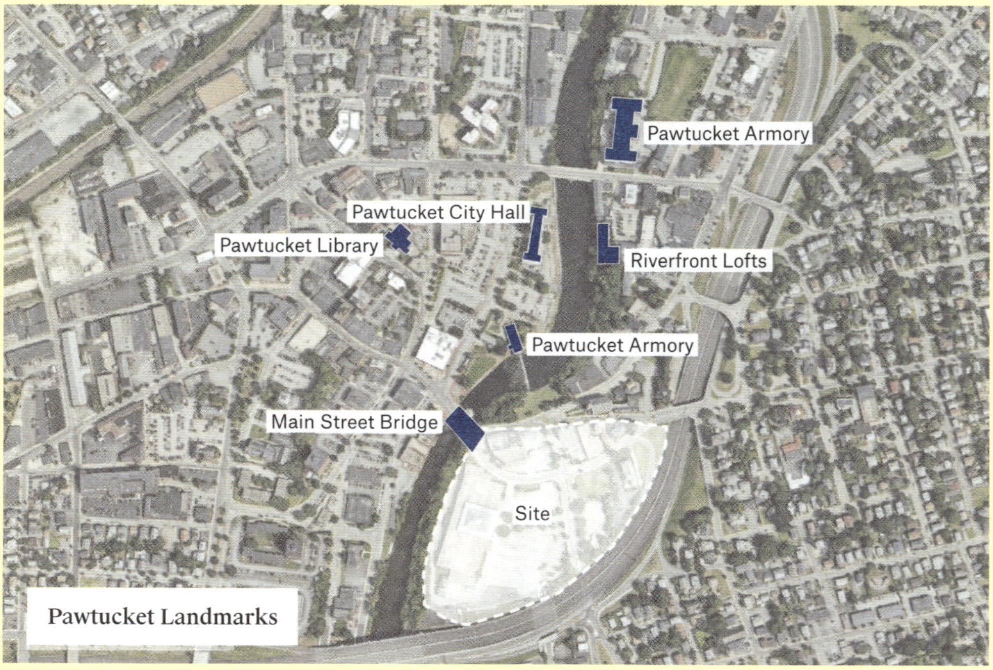
Pawtucket Armory
Pawtucket City Hall
Pawtucket Library
Riverfront Lofts
Pawtucket Armory
Main Street Bridge
Site
Pawtucket Landmarks

1.7

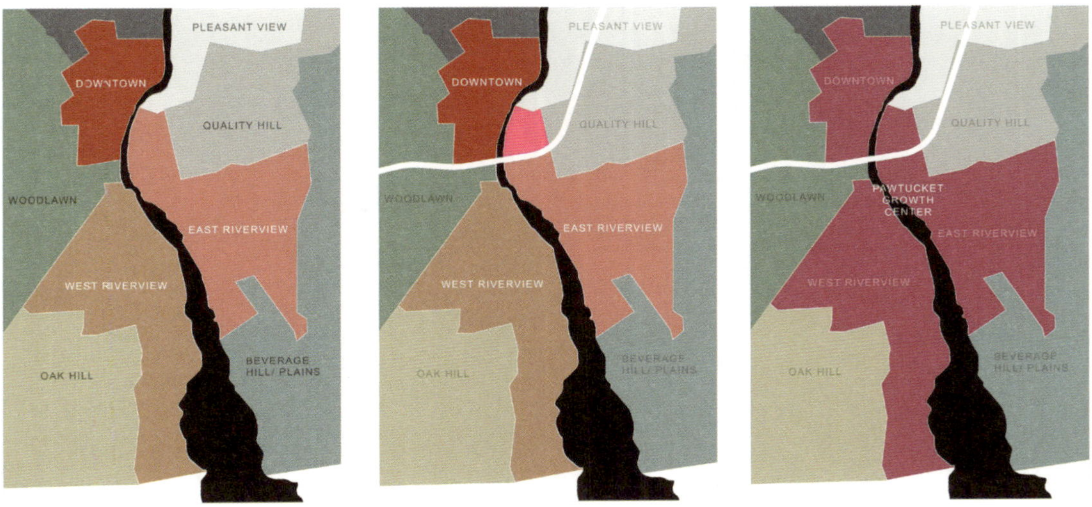

Pawtucket Neighborhoods before I-95

Pawtucket Neighborhoods after I-95

Baseball Park acting as Connector

Reconnecting Pawtucket

1.8

1.6 Diagram of the Slater Mills site and its access points.

1.7 Pawtucket landmarks close to the Slater Mills site.

1.8 The Slater Mills team's study of how Pawtucket neighborhoods could be reconnected.

1.9

1.9 Diagram of Attleboro site's entryways and points of interest.

1.10 The Attleboro team proposed infrastructure changes to support a new sports complex.

1.11 Locations of sports leagues near the Attleboro site.

1.10

1.11

Interscholastic League

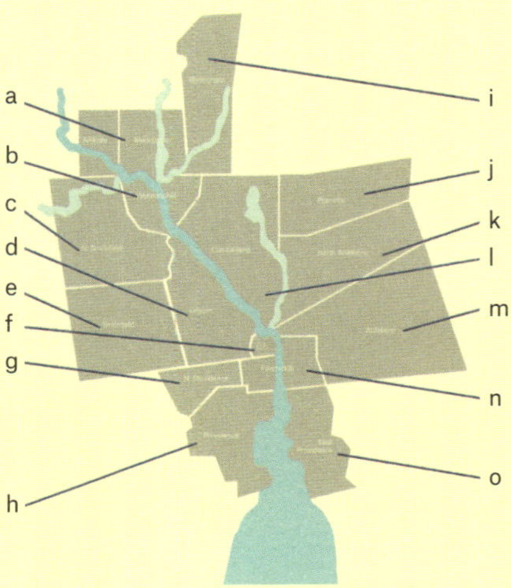

a) Blackstone-Milville High School

b) Woonsocket High School
Beacon Charter High School
Mount Saint Charles Academy

c) North Smithfield High School

d) Lincoln High School
William M. Davies Jr. Career Tech High School

e) Smithfield Senior High School
Masters Regional Academy

f) Center Falls High School

g) North Providence High School

h) Classical High School
Hope High School
Mount Pleasant High School
Central High School
Junita Sanchez High School
Dr. Jorge Alvarez High School
Moses Brown High School
Providence Career Tech Academy
La Salle Academy
Lincoln School
St. Patrick's Academy
The Wheeler School

i) Bellingham High School
Scott Hill Acres High School

j) King Philip Regional High School
Foxborough Regional Charter High School
Biship Feehan High School

k) North Attleboro High School

l) Cumberland High School
Blackstone Valley Prep Mayoral Academy

m) Attleboro High School

n) Blackstone Academy Charter School
William E. Tolman Senior High School
Charles E. Shea High School
Jacqueline M. Walsh School
Saint Raphael Academy

p) East Providence High School
Providence Country Day School
St. Mary Academy

1.12

1.12 Photo collage of existing factory buildings near the Attleboro site.

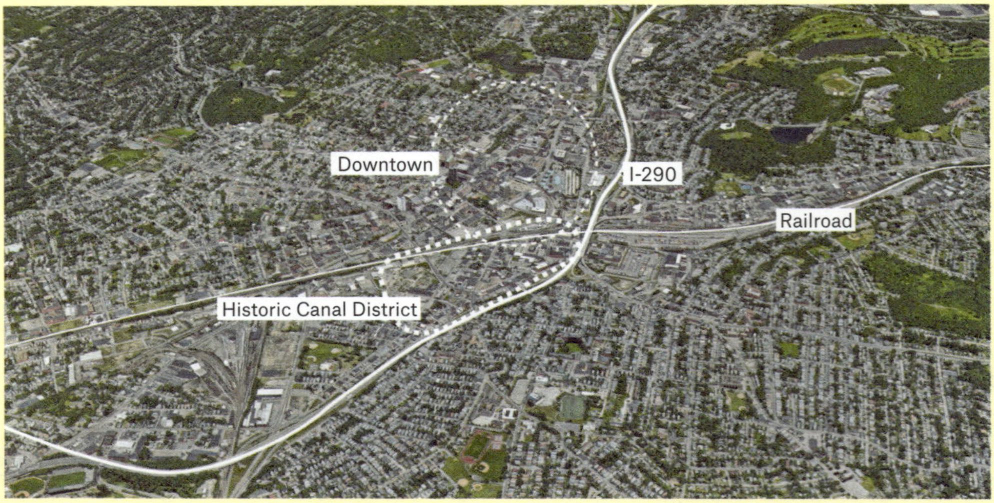

1.13

1.14

1.13 **Diagram of the Worcester site's entryways and points of interest.**

1.14 **Existing cultural landmarks near the ballpark site in Worcester.**

Team One
The Real McCoy

McCoy Stadium

Daniel Fetcho and
Ron Ostezan

As the oldest ballpark still in use in the minor-leagues, McCoy Stadium's heritage reaches beyond baseball. This project focuses on the enhancement of the existing stadium through restoration, while the addition of complementary wings and an outfield concourse bring the WPA project into the twenty-first century. Conceived as a community-oriented ballpark from the start, McCoy Stadium is located in a primarily residential area of Pawtucket, suggesting this project be developed as a "neighborhood park."

With a semicircular steel-truss canopy that covers a large seating bowl, the design of McCoy Stadium is distinctive. However, the concourse around the bowl is small, and its vomitories (entrances that pierce the stadium seating) are outdated. In the design for the retrofit of the existing structure, the concourse is extended to increase circulation space for fans and create more room for team activities below (some of which, like the practice areas and batting cages, become visible to the public). By taking out several rows of seats at the concourse level, fans standing or waiting for concessions, now have clear sight lines to the field. Concessions are placed perpendicular to the field, so as to create public pockets within the concourse. The press box has been reconfigured, with a club zone beneath, creating priority seating that the ballpark needs for increased revenue.

The goal is to transform the experience at McCoy. Today, minor-league ballparks provide lively activities for families. To accommodate those activities, an outfield addition has areas for childrens' games, interactive exhibits, special field-level access, and varying seating layouts. The concourse itself is conceived as a public path on non-game days, providing retail and concessions that are open year-round. The outfield buildings house plenty of space for community programming, offering a library, classrooms, and other areas to help facilitate community endeavors. These additions to McCoy make it not only a contemporary ballpark, but also a thriving center of the neighborhood.

2.1

2.1 Northeast-facing aerial perspective, showing proposed outfield concourse addition and connection to existing seating bowl.

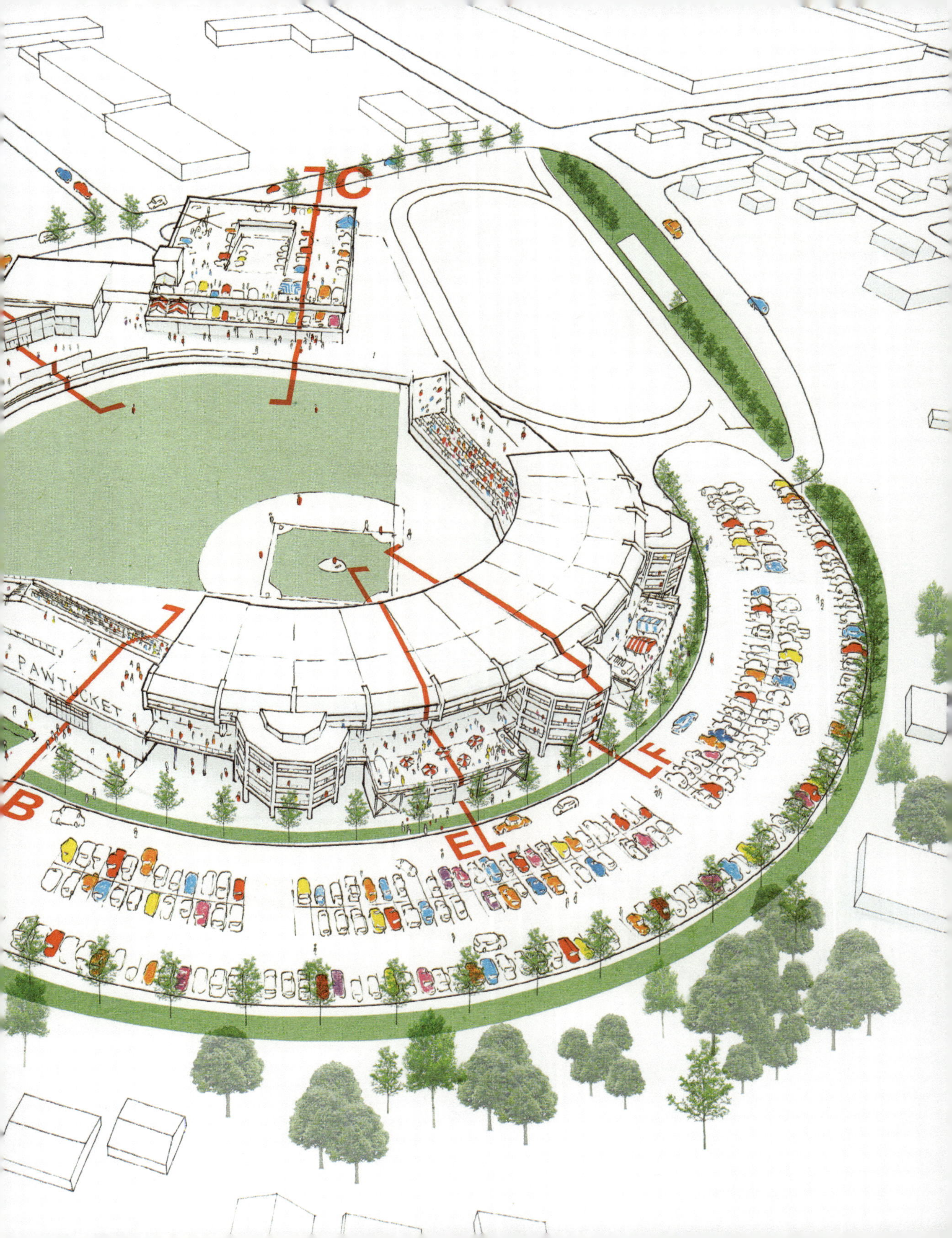

C
B
E
F
PAWTUCKET

2.2

2.3

2.4

2.2 Section through main entrance, showing game-day drop-off zone, exhibit space, party rental areas, community programming, and the outfield concourse.

2.3 Section through kid zone and secondary entrance, depicting family activities and on-grade visual access to the field.

2.4 View of the seating bowl, showing an updated press box, box seating below, and the reconfigured concourse level with standing room.

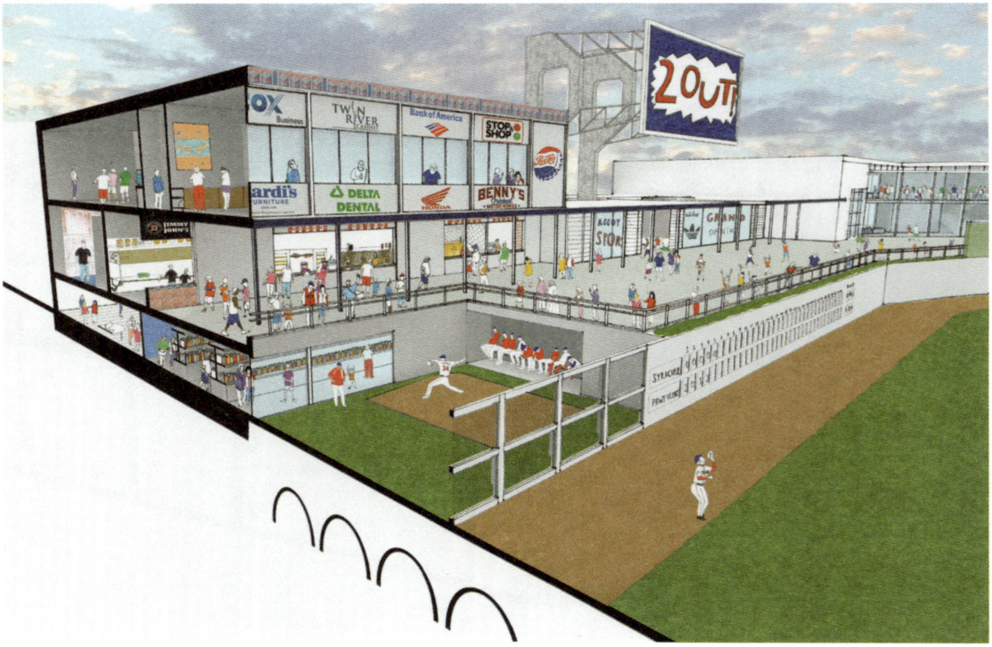

2.5

2.6

2.5 Illustration of outfield concourse, showing the bullpen, a community library, year-round stores in the outfield concourse, and team offices on the third floor.

2.6 Parking garage with space for tailgate picnics.

2.7 View of the seating bowl, showing the removal of several rows of seats and the batting cages below an enlarged concourse.

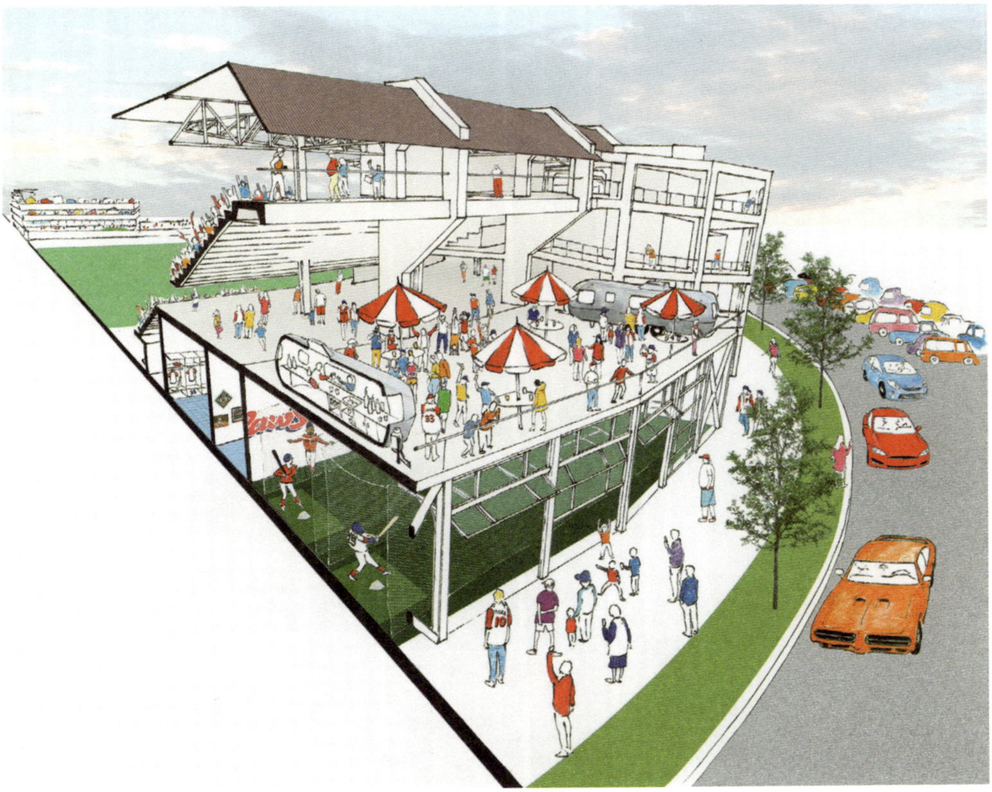

2.7

2.8 Figure-ground plan of the middle school designed on-axis with home plate of McCoy, which served to order the design of the center field buildings.

2.9 Seating chart, showing different areas of the ballpark.

2.10 Diagrams of future development of Division Street, making it the main connection to downtown Pawtucket and enlivening access to McCoy Stadium.

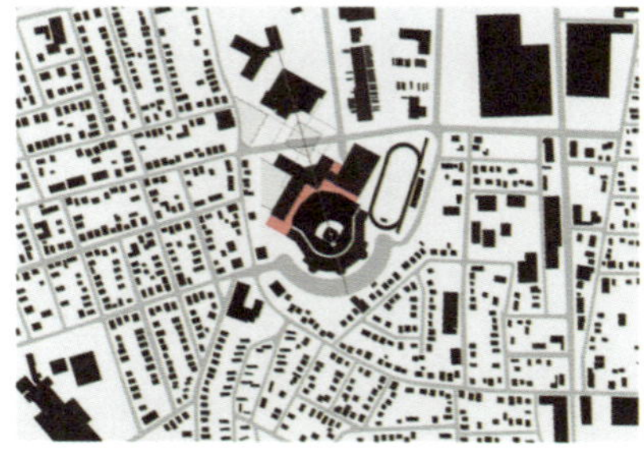

2.8

2.9

Existing Condition
5 YR. Projection
20 YR. Projection
Key
Single Family
Multi-Family
Industrial
Commercial
Firehouse

2.10

Team Two
Crosstown Connections

Slater Mill

Valeria Flores, Zachary Hoffmann, and Dylan Weiser

In response to the Pawtucket Red Sox's plan for a new ballpark, this project suggests the team remains in Pawtucket, becoming a valuable community member by making its stadium a dynamic force in the revitalization of the city's downtown. Despite being less than a mile from the team's current home, the new location puts the ballpark near the Slater Mill Historic Site, the downtown area, and the Blackstone River. The design proposal for a contemporary minor-league park takes advantage of the prime site to attract all sorts of fans.

The relocation of the ballpark reestablishes a long-forgotten relationship to the Blackstone River, which has been ignored in the city's redevelopment. Valuing the river as a natural attraction, the design offers a riverfront pedestrian walk, blurring the boundary between the stadium and the community. To further reinforce the stadium's identity as a player on the community's team, the design includes amenities–bars, restaurants, and retail–that are open to the public even in the off-season. Thus, the private enterprise of the ballpark extends into the public space of the adjacent Slater Mill neighborhood.

The design bridges not only the ballpark and Pawtucket, providing unobstructed views and visual landmarks, but also connects the neighborhoods on either side of the Blackstone River. Capitalizing on the city's proposed transit plan, the project dramatically increases the area's circulation, hoping to create new connections, increase economic activity, and revitalize Pawtucket.

3.1

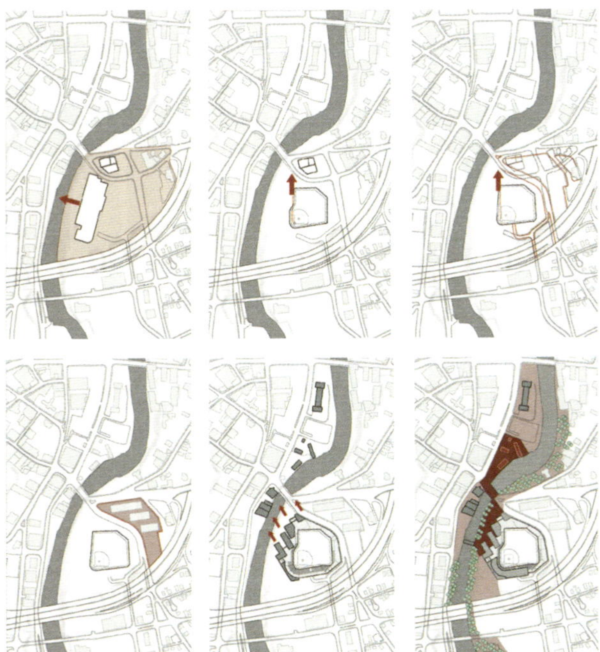

3.2

3.1 Site plan, showing connections to downtown Pawtucket and proposed development.

3.2 Planning diagrams, depicting existing conditions, desired relationships, and future growth.

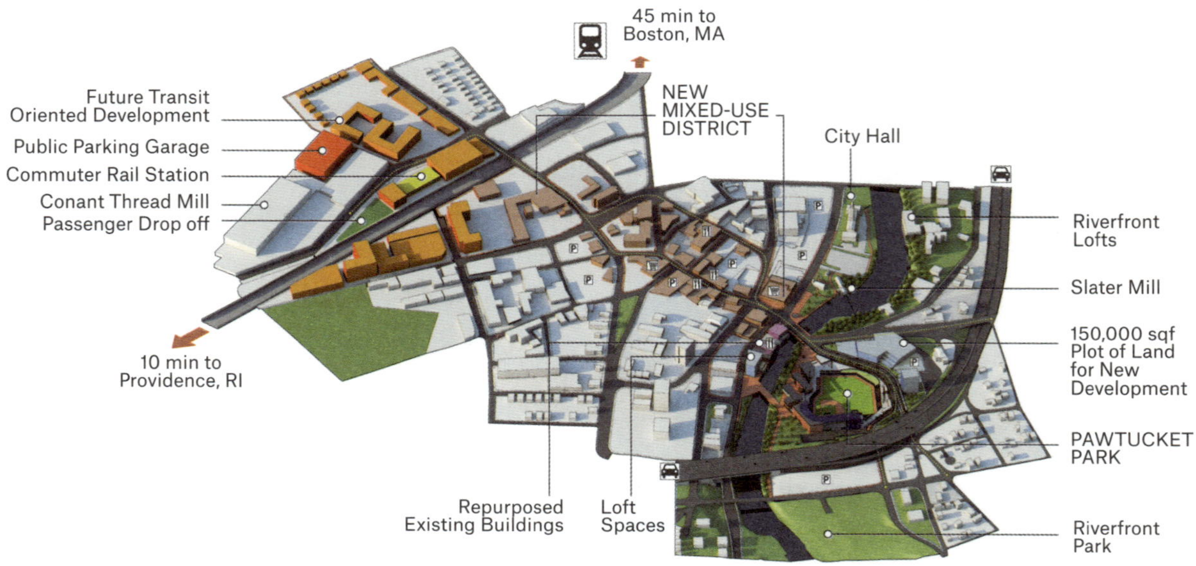
45 min to
Boston, MA
Future Transit
Oriented Development
Public Parking Garage
Commuter Rail Station
Conant Thread Mill
Passenger Drop off
NEW
MIXED-USE
DISTRICT
City Hall
Riverfront
Lofts
Slater Mill
150,000 sqf
Plot of Land
for New
Development
PAWTUCKET
PARK
Riverfront
Park
10 min to
Providence, RI
Repurposed
Existing Buildings
Loft
Spaces

3.3

3.4

3.3 Axonometric drawing, showing a revitalized downtown and the new ballpark's surrounding areas.

3.4 Perspective from across the Blackstone River, looking toward the main entrance to the new ballpark.

3.5

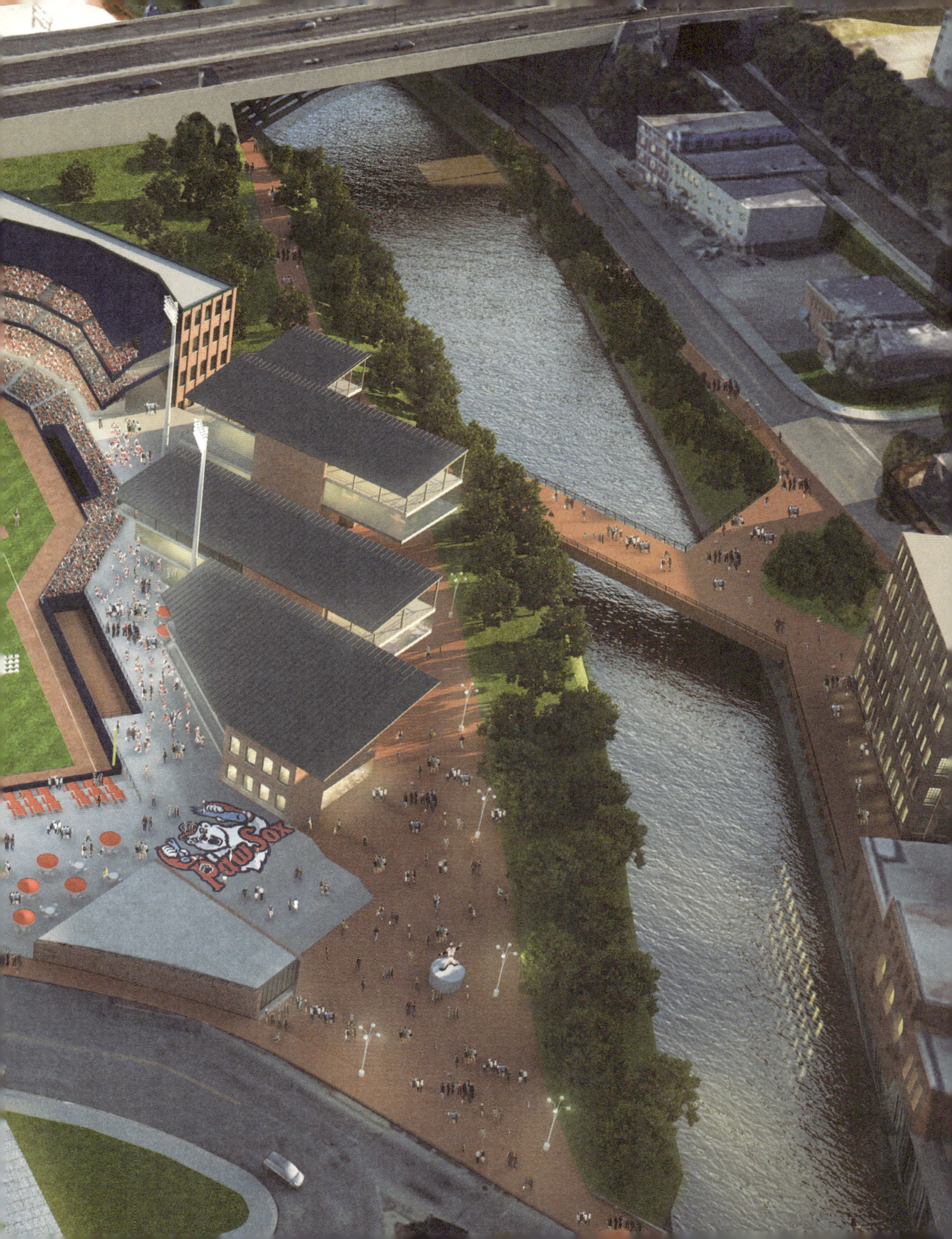
PawSox

3.6

3.5 (previous spread) **South-facing aerial perspective, showing an active zone along the river.**

3.6 **Bird's-eye perspective, looking northwest.**

3.7 **Ground-level perspective, looking toward entrance and outfield buildings.**

3.7

3.8

3.9

3.8 **Model, looking northwest.**

3.9 **Model, looking south.**

Team Three

Titanium: A Ballfield and a Sports Campus

Attleboro

Heewon Choi, Audrey Yifei Li, and Christine Tran

Located on land that was once occupied by the Howard and Bullough American Machine Company, our proposed site is positioned between three cities: Pawtucket and Central Falls, Rhode Island, and Attleboro, Massachusetts. With this context in mind, our team conceived of the ballpark as a potential catalyst for collaboration among the three cities; this vision led to a highly diverse project that, in itself and in its effects, provides mutual benefits to all.

To achieve this vision, the team offers a speculative regional master plan, not just a ballpark design. Anchoring the project on the Blackstone River as the center of a sports campus, the team responded to the regional need for interscholastic league sports facilities that would be used year-round for athletes at all levels, expanding the typical baseball stadium calendar. An existing industrial shed is reimagined off right field to accommodate private clubs, standing-room areas, concessions, and services. To further underline the region's identity, the design uses the old factory's iconic smokestack to create a new entrance to Boomers Park.

This proposal envisions a highly diversified development, including K–12 tournament stadiums, playing fields, a riverfront park, residential complexes, and hotels—all of which will provide economic benefits and a sustainable future for the region. To complement this vision, the Pawtucket Red Sox would be rebranded as the Blackstone Boomers, honoring these three cities' industrial past while establishing a new identity for the region as a recreational corridor.

GO BOOMERS!

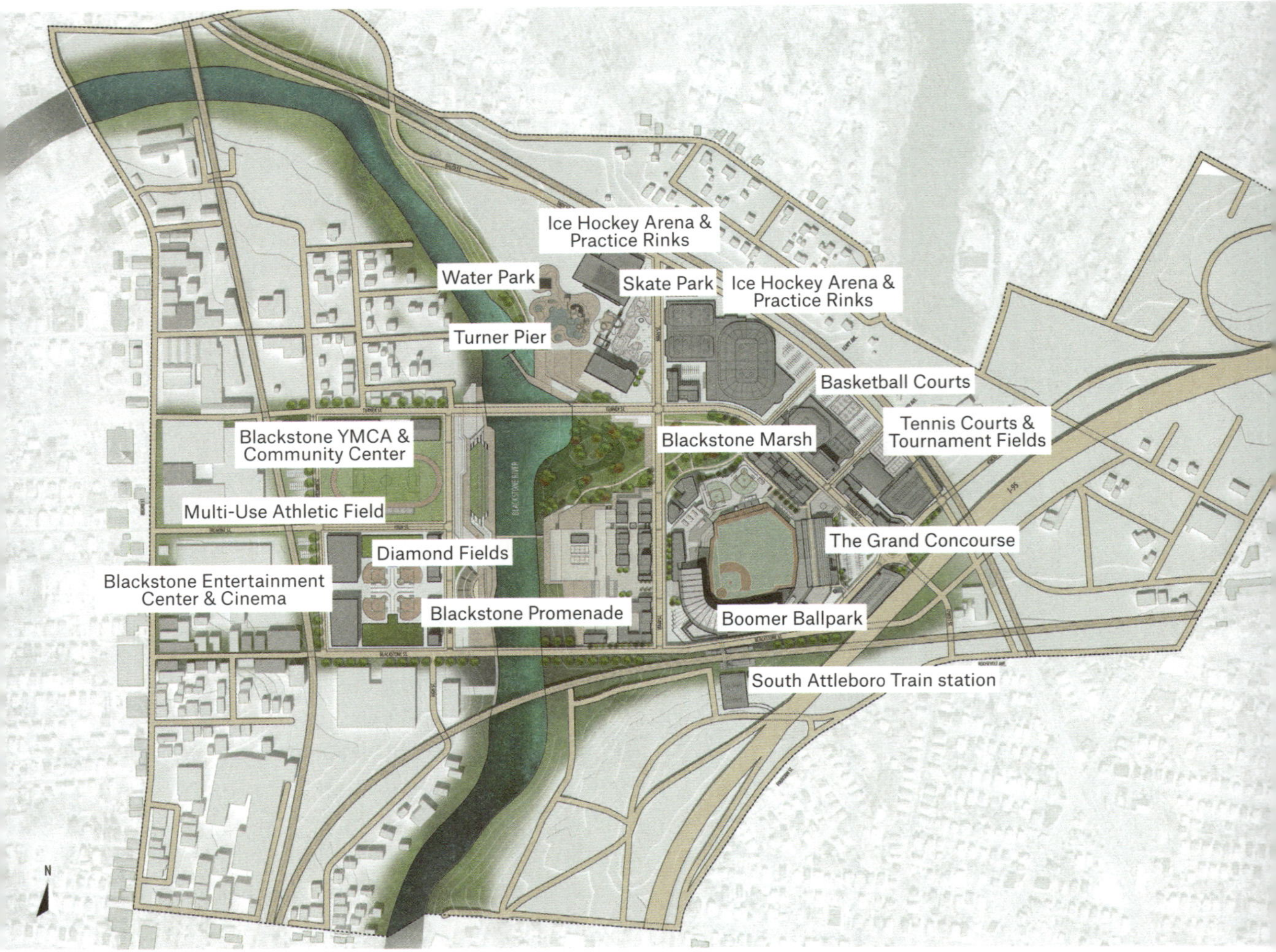
Ice Hockey Arena &
Practice Rinks
Water Park
Skate Park
Ice Hockey Arena &
Practice Rinks
Turner Pier
Basketball Courts
Tennis Courts &
Tournament Fields
Blackstone YMCA &
Community Center
Blackstone Marsh
Multi-Use Athletic Field
The Grand Concourse
Diamond Fields
Blackstone Entertainment
Center & Cinema
Blackstone Promenade
Boomer Ballpark
South Attleboro Train station
N

4.1

Blackstone
Boomers
25
B
BLACKSTONE

4.2

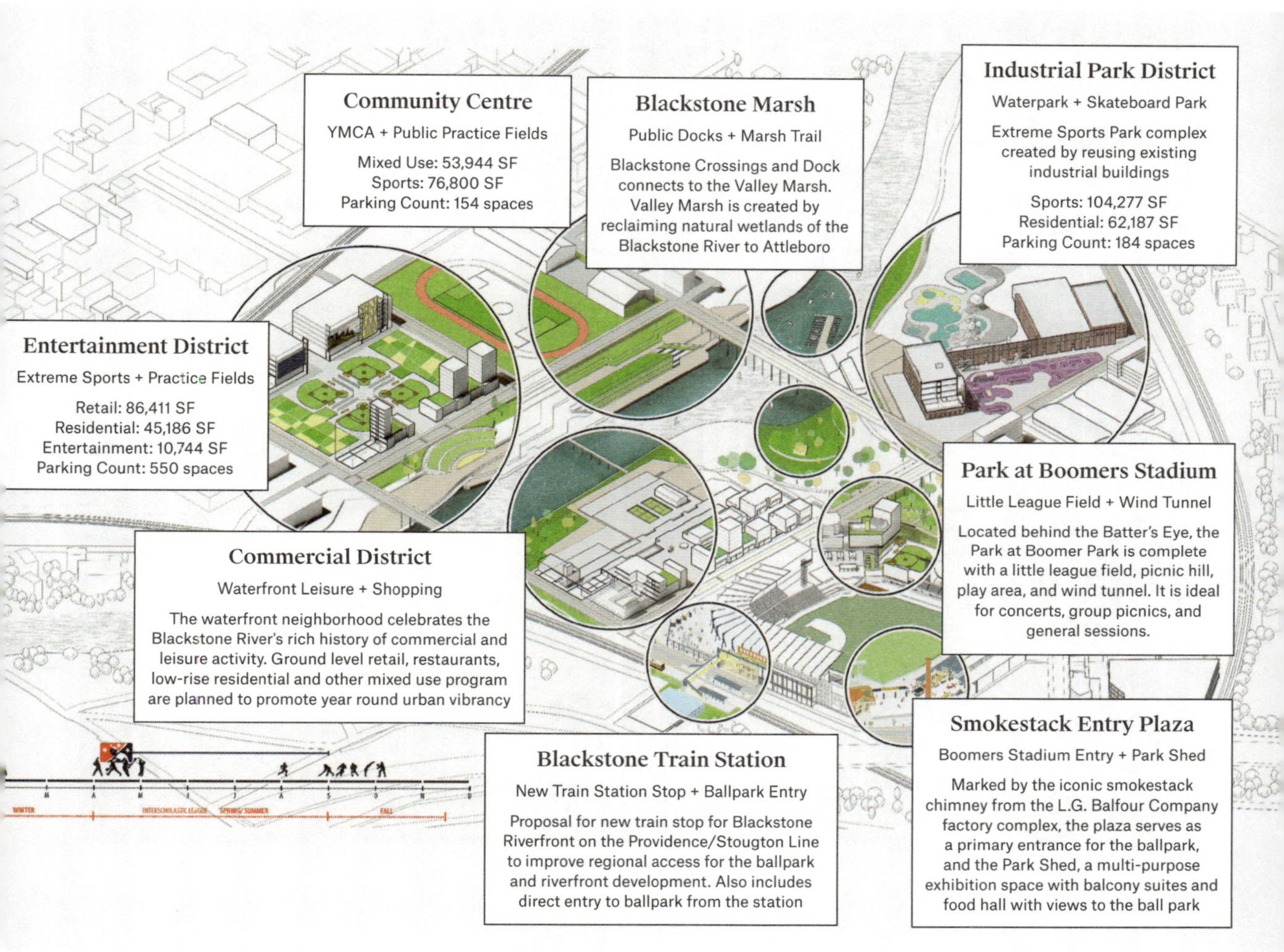

4.3

4.1 Site plan, showing proposed development and infrastructure.

4.2 New team branding of the Blackstone Boomers.

4.3 Axonometric drawing, depicting sports facilities within the larger proposed complex.

Boomers Park
AT BLACKSTONE CROSSING
Diamond club seats
Super club seats
Field box seats
Club seats
Box Seats
1. VIP suites
2. Media room
3. Picnic terrace
4. Third base pavilion
5. Kid's zone & family park
6. Third base bleachers and berm
7. Tournament clubhouses
8. Youth sports zone & pick-up softball fields
9. Centerfield berm
10. Birthday & team party porch
11. Grand food concourse / public art gallery
12. Reserved club decks
13. South Attleboro train station
box office
information kiosk
parking
food
beverage
team store
first aid
elevator
restroom
handicapped area
Gate A
Gate B
Gate C
Main St.
Blackstone St.
Exit
Exit

4.4

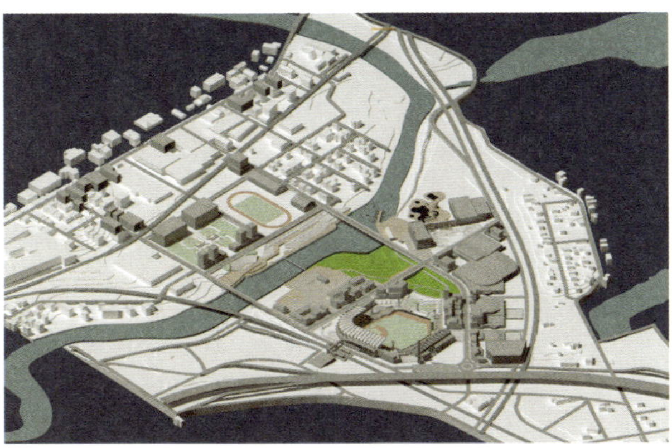

4.5

4.6

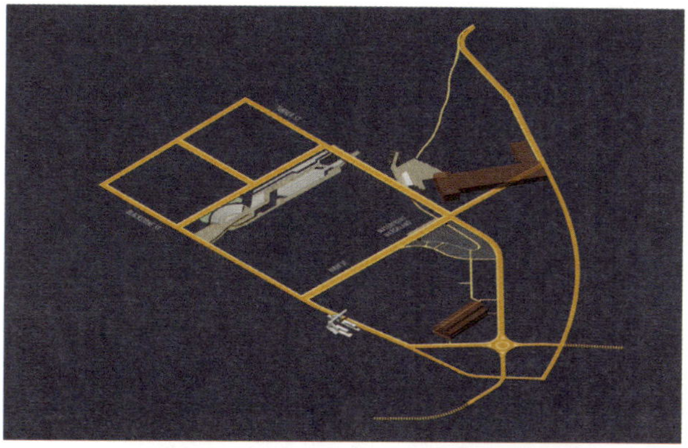

4.7

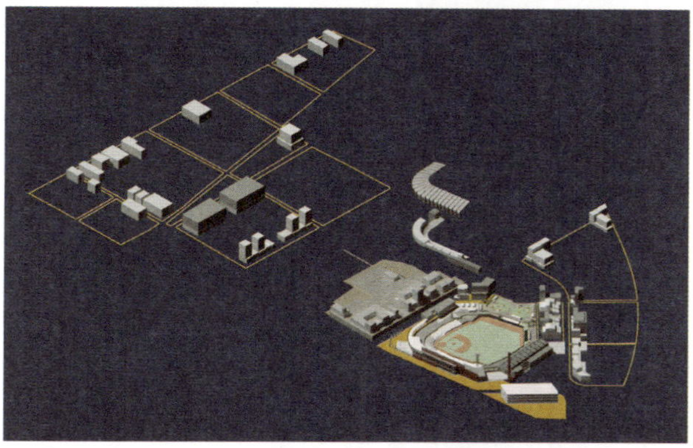

4.8

4.4 Stadium directory, showing different seating and activity areas within the new ballpark.

4.5 Axonometric drawing, showing the sports campus and ballpark situated along major transportation networks.

4.6 Phase one of the project introduces infrastructure and prepares the sites for construction.

4.7 Phase two coincides with the construction of the ballpark and adjacent buildings.

4.8 Phase three completes the project with auxiliary sports facilities.

4.9

4.9 Perspective view from seats, looking into the outfield.

4.10

4.10 West-facing aerial perspective, showing the repurposed warehouse building and the original smokestack as a point of entrance.

Team Four
Activating the Canal District

Worcester

Justin Lai and Jiajian Min

At the time of the studio, the Pawtucket Red Sox were considering moving to Worcester, Massachusetts, a more urban site than its previous location. Located in Worcester's Canal District, the proposed ballpark design integrates into the neighborhood, especially Green Street, a corridor of burgeoning economic development. Through its strategic orientation, the ballpark creates three new public zones: North Park, the Food Hall, and the Walk of Fame. The design creates areas for game-day and year-round activities, stitching together these spaces with improved circulation. Further, the controlled access allows the ballpark to expand beyond its own footprint. Sectional relationships are emphasized to maximize views into the field from the street and toward downtown and the elevated train tracks. Ultimately, the ballpark takes advantage of a promising site to be a catalyst for the entire neighborhood. Its success lies in fully integrating itself into the Canal District for real and sustainable growth for the future.

5.1 **Site plan, showing the new ballpark's connection to the city and its resulting development.**

5.2 **Ground-floor plan of the ballpark.**

5.3 (overleaf) **Axonometric drawing, depicting regional connections and surrounding points of interest.**

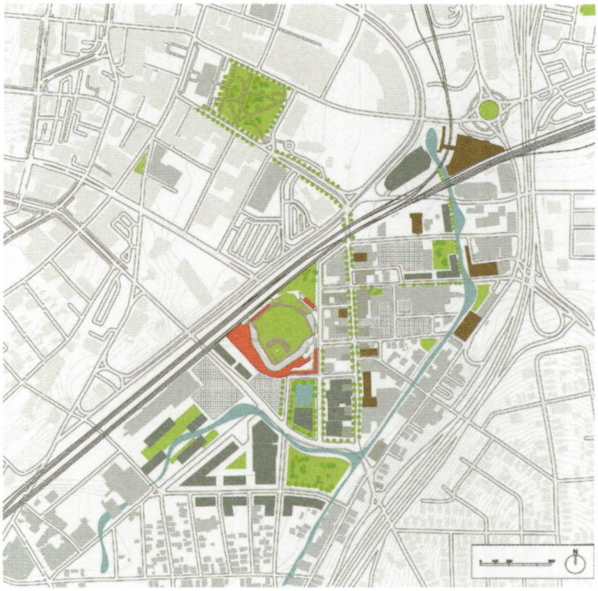

5.1

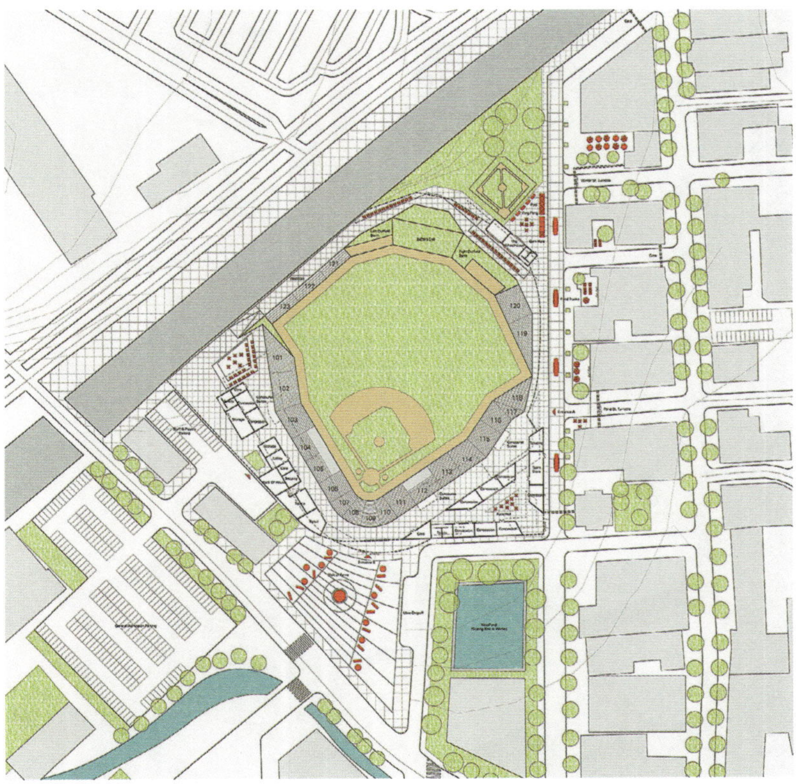

5.2

The Worcester Red Sox Stadium and Canal District

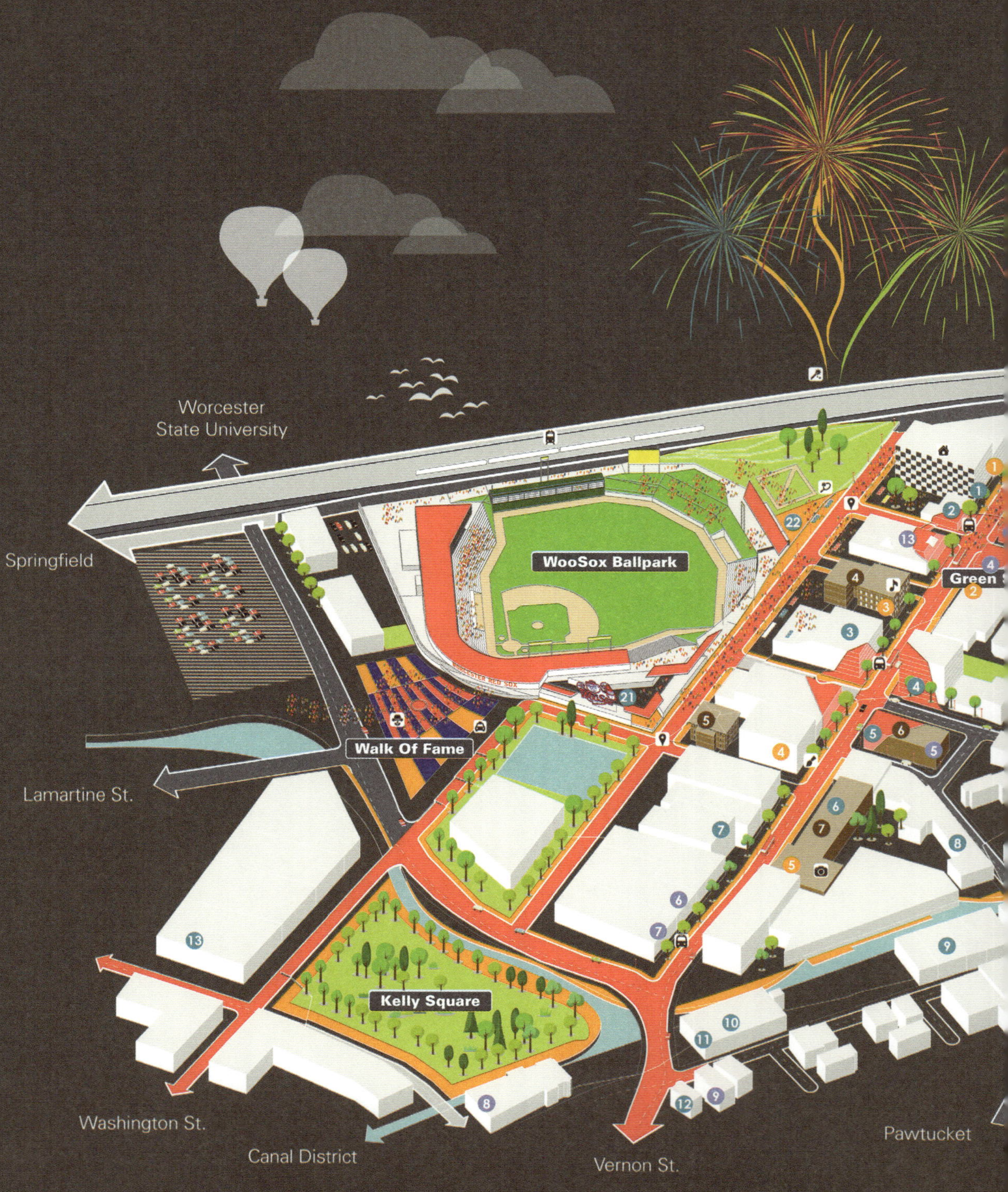

Downtown Worcester
Athol
UMass
Shrewsbury St.
Boston
Oak Hill
Station
Winter St.

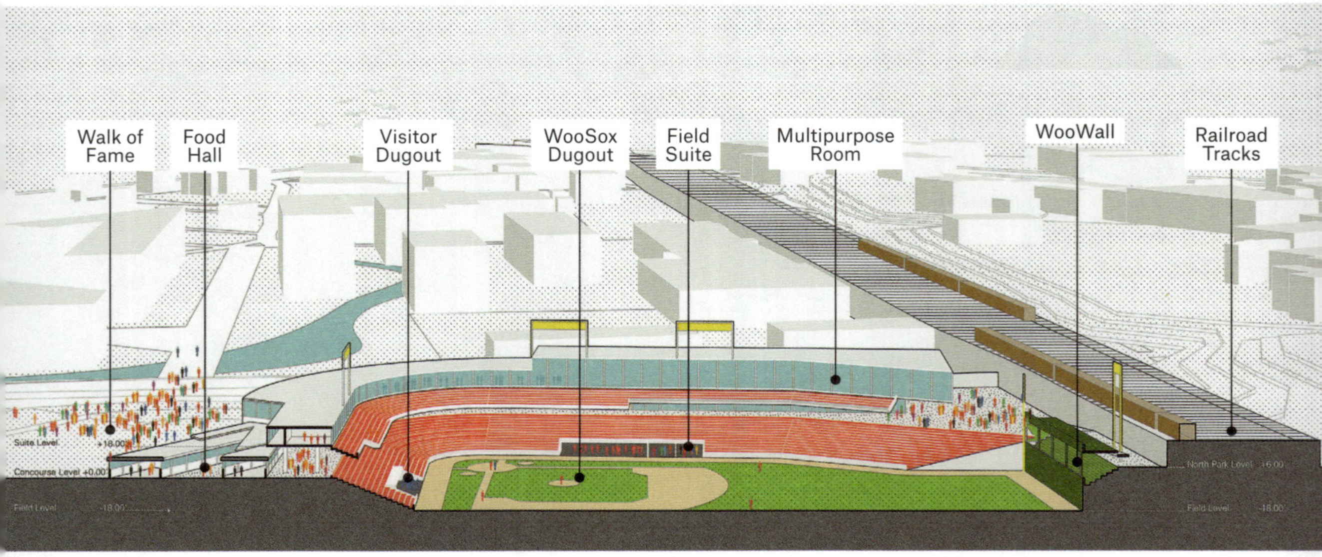
Walk of Fame
Food Hall
Visitor Dugout
WooSox Dugout
Field Suite
Multipurpose Room
WooWall
Railroad Tracks
Suite Level +18.00'
Concourse Level +0.00'
Field Level -18.00'
North Park Level +6.00'
Field Level -18.00'

5.4

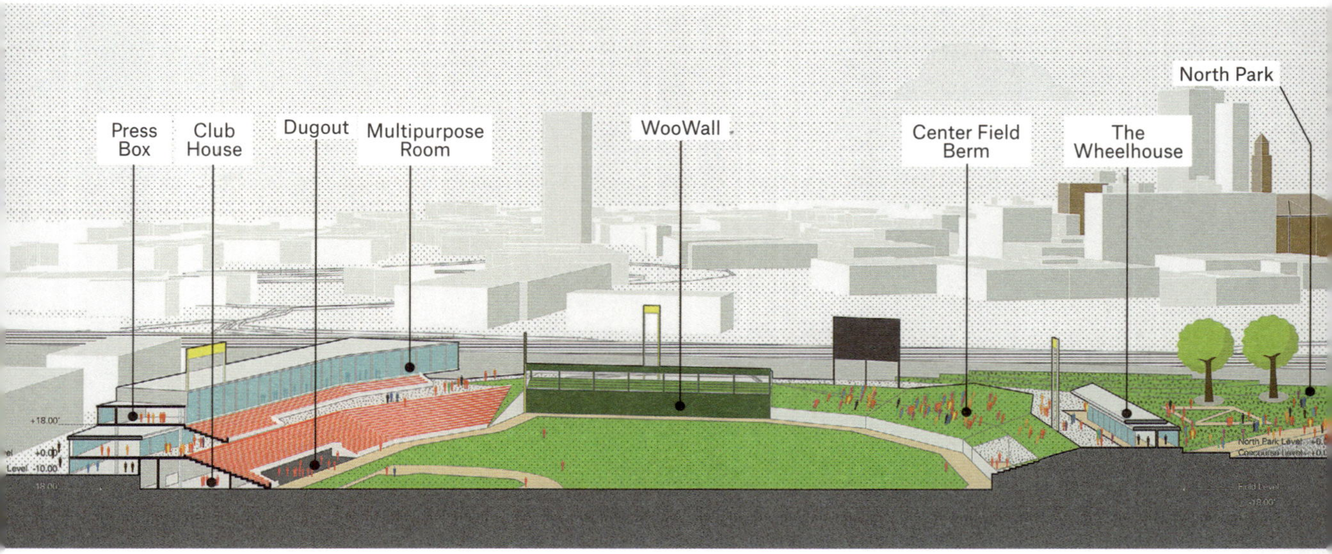

5.5

5.4 **Southwest-facing section, showing grade change and the adjacent railroad.**

5.5 **Northwest-facing section, showing urban connections around the ballpark.**

5.6 (overleaf) **Aerial perspective, looking north.**

5.6

WooSox

5.7

5.8

5.9

5.10

5.7 South-facing aerial perspective, showing access to the ballpark and activity areas.

5.8 Perspective, looking toward entrance of the ballpark.

5.9 Perspective view from seats, showing the unique outfield walls and urban context of Worcester.

5.10 Perspective, looking toward WooSox Alley and showing the ground-level sequence of arrival.

Seventh-Inning Stretch

Los Angeles Dodgers

The studio's second half focused on Dodger Stadium. Working in three teams, the students collaborated on a renovation scheme for the existing stadium as well as a new addition adjacent to centerfield. Opened in 1962, Dodger Stadium is symmetrical and includes innovative, corrugated-metal roofs and hexagonal scoreboards, but the facility is engulfed by expansive parking lots, made famous in Ed Ruscha's 1967 photograph *1000 Elysian Park Ave*. This part of the studio brief reflected a real project and its objectives, as outlined by Stan Kasten and Janet Marie Smith, who framed and grounded the students design work. While Dodger Stadium offers a range of amenities—bullpen overlooks, tremendous views, foul-line clubs, memorabilia zones, and the former 76 gas station in the centerfield-adjacent parking lot, among others—the studio emphasized improved circulation, attracting younger fans, and developing year-round activities. In the context of a stadium that, in 2017, attracted almost four million people, the studio hoped to celebrate the team's history, increase revenue, and add food and other amenities.

opposite top **View toward centerfield from the parking lot beyond Dodger Stadium.**

opposite bottom **Students in the right-field pavilion during a tour of Dodger Stadium.**

Site Research

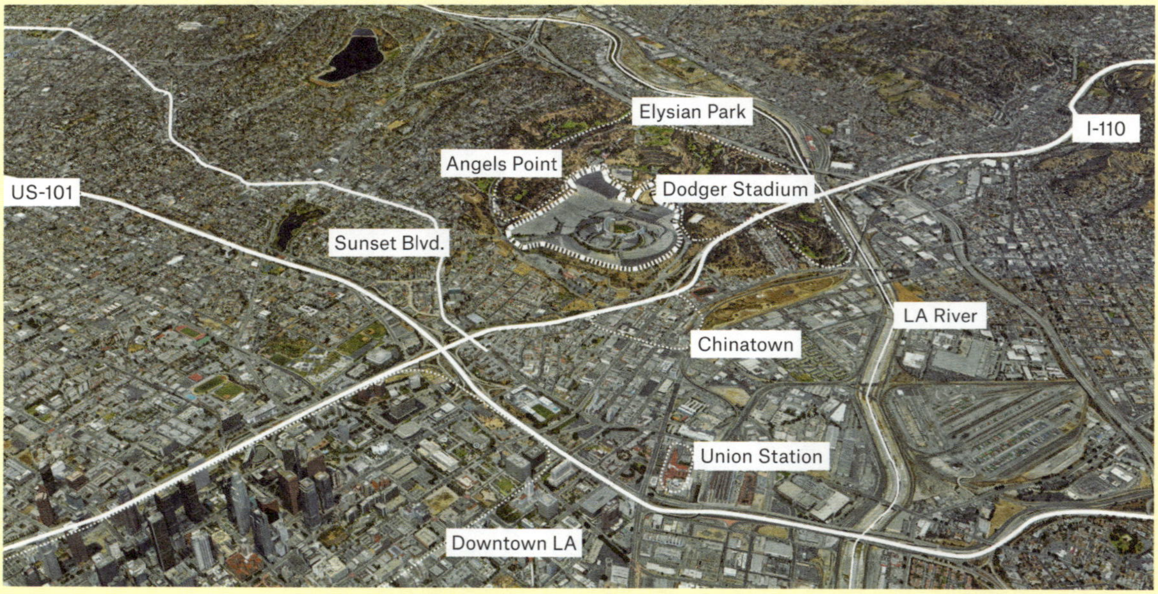

6.1

6.1 Diagram of Dodger Stadium's access and points of interest.

6.2 Vehicular entrances to Dodger Stadium.

Academy
GATE D
Golden State
GATE C
Downtown
GATE E
Stadium W
GATE B
Sunset
GATE A

6.2

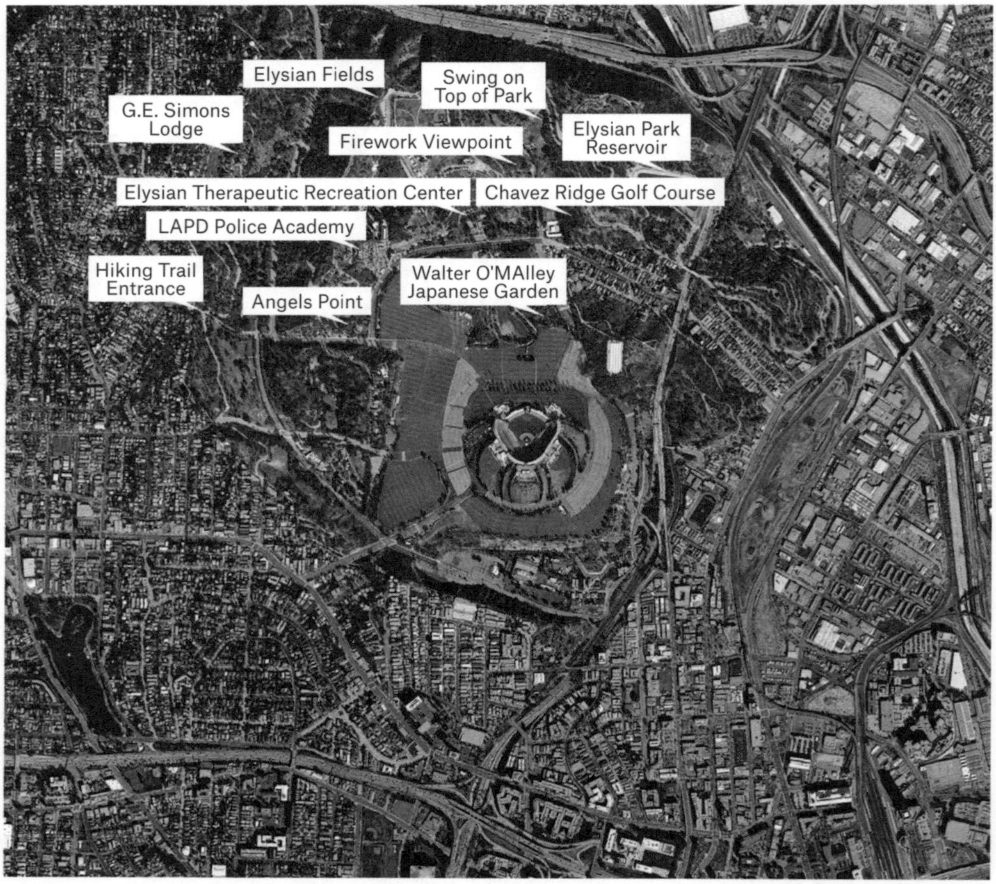
Elysian Fields
Swing on Top of Park
G.E. Simons Lodge
Firework Viewpoint
Elysian Park Reservoir
Elysian Therapeutic Recreation Center
Chavez Ridge Golf Course
LAPD Police Academy
Hiking Trail Entrance
Walter O'MAlley Japanese Garden
Angels Point

6.3

6.3 Points of interest in Elysian Park, northeast of Dodger Stadium.

6.4 Points of interest in Chinatown, south of Dodger Stadium.

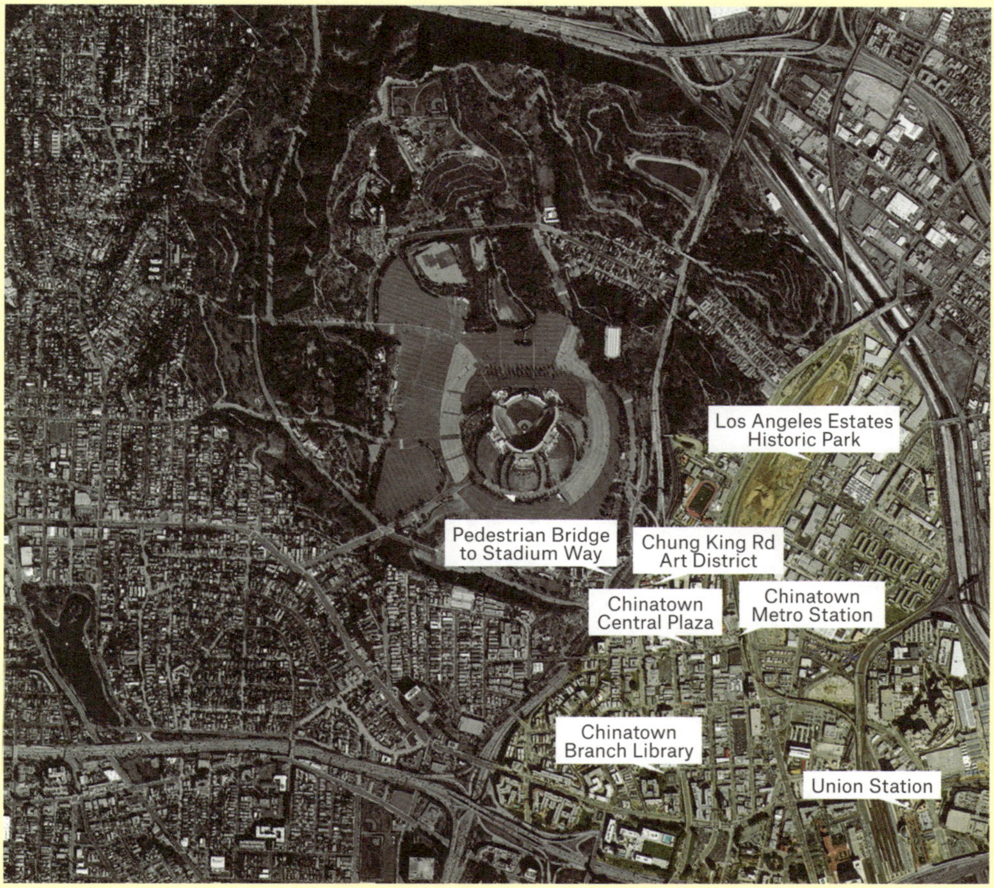

6.4

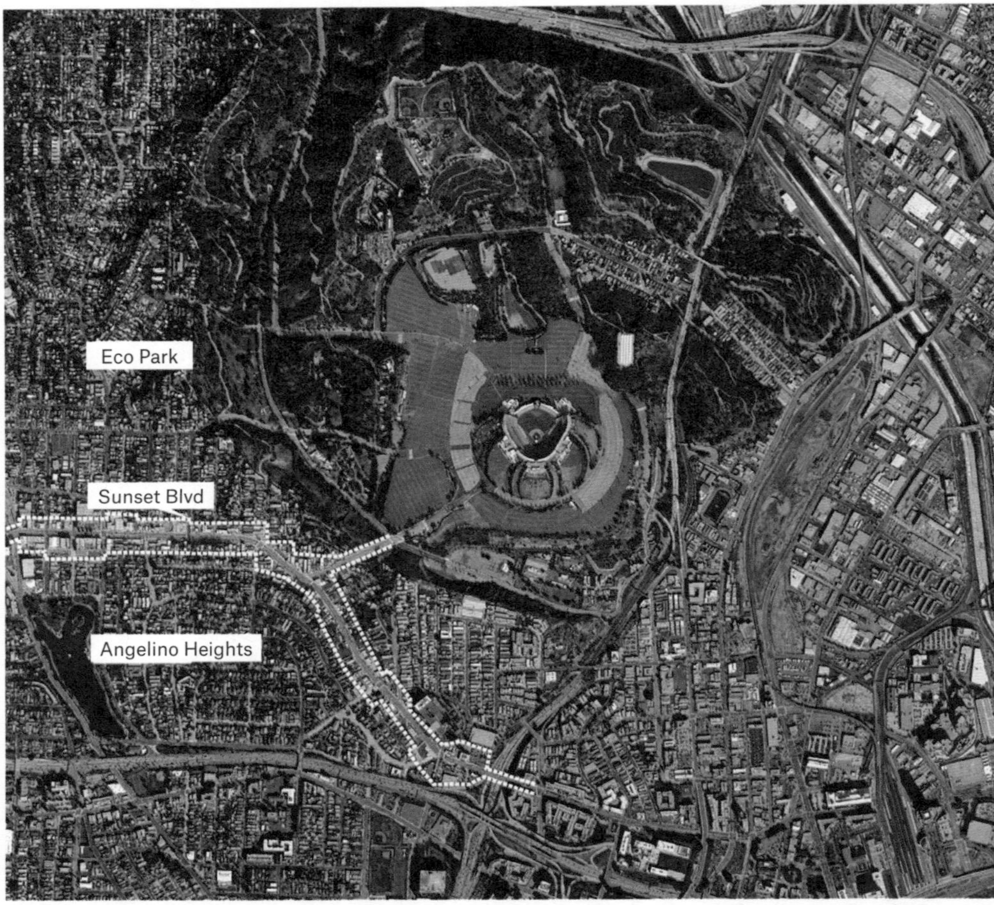

6.5

6.5 **Route of Sunset Boulevard in relation to Dodger Stadium.**

Team One
Designing the Dodger Experience

Valeria Flores, Zachary Hoffmann, and Dylan Weiser

Carved out of Chavez Ravine's landscape, Dodger Stadium has dramatic grade changes. Today, there is a disjointed fan experience between the point of arrival, entry to the ballpark, and arrival to seats. This proposal for a new centerfield area embraces the site's topography and reinstates Dodger Stadium as a hospitable landscape for fans to have a new and improved game-day experience.

The game-day sequence begins with a new public transportation arrival point, where the Dodgers Express line drops off fans at the entrance to what this design team calls "The Dodger Experience." This tactic provides Dodger-themed amenities, from landscape features (such as terraced beds and shaped pots) and statues to new museum areas in the ballpark. A simulated, below-grade "clubhouse" lets fans take the same processional path as the baseball players, moving from the dugout and into the reimagined centerfield area.

In this new centerfield area, visitors can move through the museums or cross on a raised walkway, which connects to the existing concourse level. On this level, fans find the ticket booths and team store, along with a series of amenities (bars and restaurants) and entertainment (fan lookouts and photo opportunities). These experiences are enhanced by a clear view of the game through the redesigned Batter's Eye, which currently is just a black tarp around the loud speakers. A standard ballpark element, the black Batter's Eye provides a contrast to the white baseball, allowing batters to see the ball being thrown. To augment this experience, the students designed operable shutters that can open between innings, expanding the view through the Batter's Eye.

The visual porosity is also found in carved-out spaces in the existing bleachers; these spaces use extended balconies for new and expanded fan congregations. At the top of the newly designed landscape, a terrace includes gathering spaces, bars, and views onto the field and into Elysian Park.

7.1 Aerial perspective, showing proposed Dodger Stadium center-field addition and the reimagined drop-off area behind the existing outfield pavilions.

7.2 Perspective, showing the new outfield entry to Dodger Stadium.

7.3 Perspective of the new outfield concourse area behind the existing pavilions, with the new Batter's Eye Club in centerfield.

7.1

Spectrum
Dodgers
THE DODGER EXPERIENCE
LET'S GO
DODGERS!

7.2

Mercedes-Benz
BATTER'S EYE CLUB
24
53
42

7.3

7.4

7.4 Section perspective, depicting entry sequence and large museum behind the Batter's Eye.

7.5 Field-facing perspective view looking from above the proposed Batter's Eye Club.

7.5

7.6

7.6 View, looking toward center-field from the top deck of Dodger Stadium.

7.7 Aerial view of proposed center-field addition, with programmed areas behind the Batter's Eye.

Spectrum
HISTORY OF THE DODGER UNIFORM
LET'S GO
DODGERS!
Fly Emirates
Budweiser
THIS BUD'S FOR YOU.
Bank of America

7.7

7.8

7.8 **Perspective view within the Dodgers' Hall of Fame in centerfield.**

7.9 **Northwest-facing view of sectional model.**

7.9

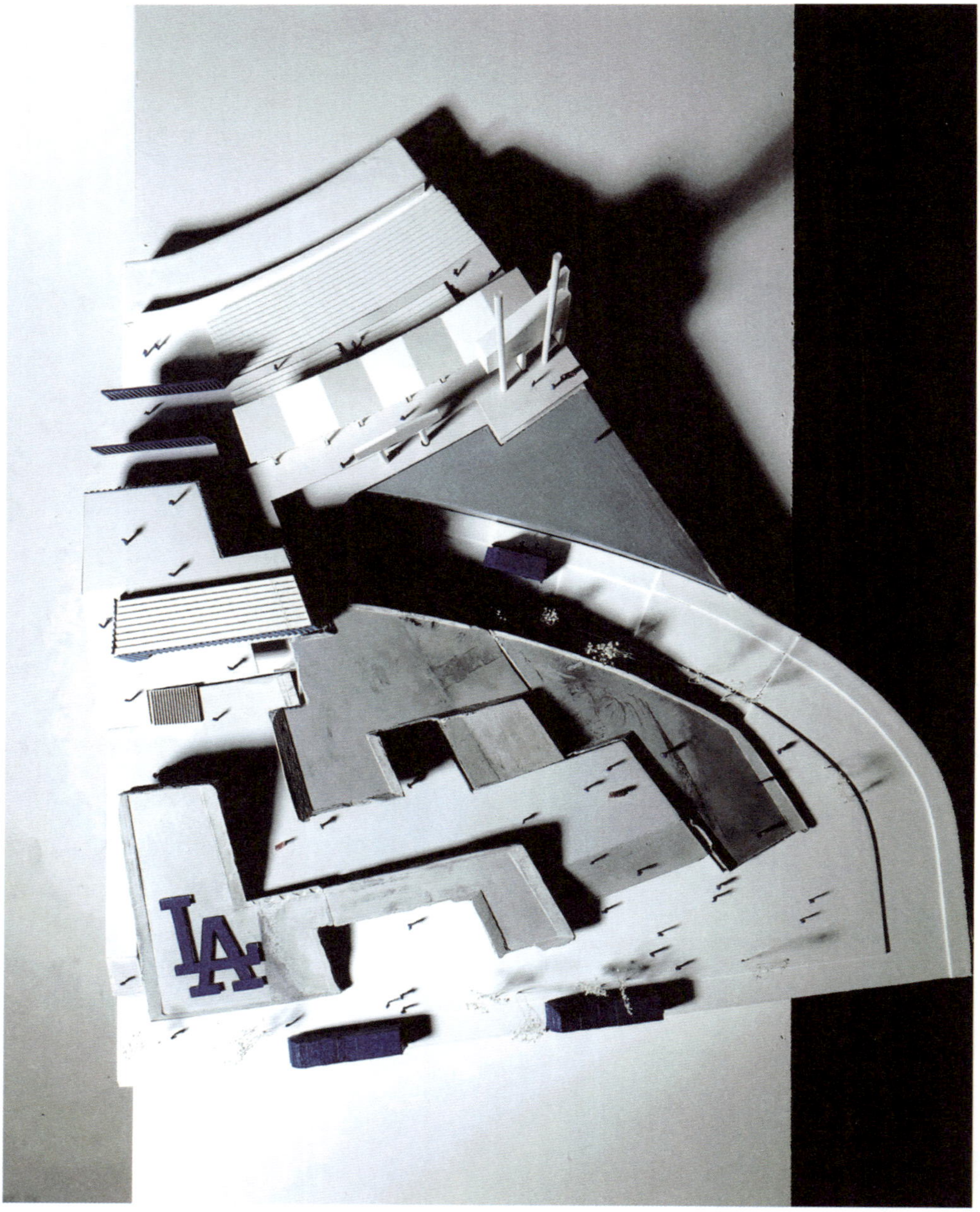

7.10

7.10 **Bird's-eye view of model.**

Team Two
Dodger Stadium on the Sunset Ring

Audrey Yifei Li, Jiajian Min, and Christine Tran

Dodger Stadium was conceived at the height of U.S. automobile consumption, which encouraged drive-through restaurants, drive-in movie theaters, and other car-based businesses. As the link between Los Angeles and the Pacific Ocean, Sunset Boulevard exemplifies this shift and now is central to the city's identity. Approximately twenty-two miles long, the boulevard abruptly ends just south of Dodger Stadium. Inspired by Ed Ruscha's "Every Building on the Sunset Strip" 1962 essay, the project emphasizes the importance of architecture, signage, and the automobile to L.A. culture. Reimagining Dodger Stadium as the beginning of Sunset Boulevard, this design enhances that particular street in the urban landscape.

This proposal creates a "Sunset Ring" to integrate the park and the stadium. To knit together these two disparate territories, a landscaped intervention is positioned in front of centerfield, creating a green front door to the stadium. The intervention is divided into three petals, each of which takes on a different character to merge Elysian Park with Sunset Boulevard. The Park Petal allows Elysian Park to flow toward right field and accommodates picnic areas, Whiffle-ball diamonds, and event space. The Center Petal celebrates car culture by reestablishing a drive-in movie theater where ticket holders can watch a movie and eat. Designed after historical precedents and reimagined with the Dodgers' past in mind, lights and signage line the ballpark's Vin Scully Avenue as a direct extension of Sunset Boulevard. Terminating at the Entry Petal, the drop-off plaza leads to the largest sign of all: the back of the Dodger Stadium scoreboard, which marks the park's new entry pavilion.

8.1

8.1 **All-Star Game map, depicting "Fanfest" activities and the redesigned centerfield area of Dodger Stadium.**

8.2 Perspective view, showing the outfield entry to Dodger Stadium and a large scoreboard that faces to the parking lot.

8.3 Perspective view, depicting new activity areas beyond the outfield pavilions.

8.2

8.3

8.4

8.4 Perspective view, depicting the drive-in movie's parking lot with screens for viewing baseball on game days and films during other times of the year.

8.5 Extension of Sunset Boulevard into the parking lot of Dodger Stadium.

8.5

8.6

8.6 Night perspective, showing Sunset Boulevard's connection to the stadium and the new activity zones behind the outfield bleachers.

8.7 Perspective view, showing the proposed outfield concourse's new paths of circulation and food and beverage spots.

8.8 View of the proposed Hall of Fame museum, located underneath the outfield pavilions.

8.7

8.8

8.9 Site plan, indicating new park areas behind centerfield and reimagined vehicular circulation within the parking lot.

8.10 Foldout diagram of historic Dodger signage and its use on the new Sunset Boulevard extension into the stadium.

8.9

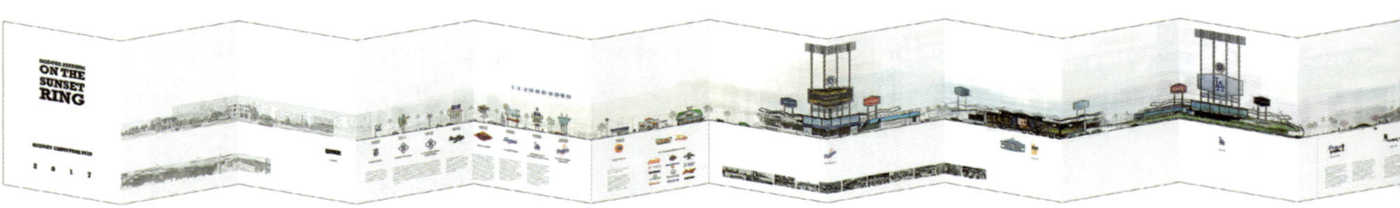

8.10

Team Three
Blue Street at Dodger Stadium

Heewon Choi, Daniel Fetcho, Justin Lai, and Ron Ostezan

This project proposes a new centerfield building, elevated pedestrian paths, and, situated behind Dodger Stadium's existing outfield bleachers, an open-air corridor, Blue Street. Connecting to existing concourse levels, Blue Street is a destination for fans before, during, and after the game, offering baseball-related experiences, exciting concessions and retailers, and easier access between levels and around the stadium.

Blue Street creates a large public space, which the current stadium lacks. This idea satisfies the need for a second major entrance (by connecting to the networks of Elysian Park, Chinatown, and Sunset Boulevard) and reconceptualizes the fan experience (through engaging exhibitions, food and retail, and clear wayfinding). Blue Street houses a food court, children's games, exhibits, retail, and food and beverage. The critical mass of novelty shops allows the street to operate on non-game days, attracting fans and revenue throughout the year. Elevated pedestrian bridges to Elysian Park and other important destinations leave the lower level open for vehicle circulation.

Responding to the Dodgers' desire for a Hall of Fame within the ballpark and the capacity to host large concerts and events, the project includes a new centerfield building and Batter's Eye. The ground level hosts temporary exhibitions that allow services and equipment onto the field. On the second level, a tinted-glass Batter's Eye provides views to the field, while a museum displays exhibitions on conveyor belts under glass floors; the museum also houses holographs and A/R and V/R walls that make for innovative attractors. Once again Dodger Stadium will revolutionize the concept of the fan experience at a baseball park.

9.1

9.2

9.1 (previous spread) **Aerial perspective, showing the Blue Street addition and the different physical connections it creates.**

9.2 **Perspective view of the drop-off zone and new centerfield entry with a footbridge.**

9.3 Perspective view toward Dodger Stadium from Elysian Park, showing a reconfigured ring road, adjusted parking zones, and the centerfield addition beyond.

9.3

9.4 Perspective view of Blue Street, looking down from an upper level that connects to the existing bleachers in the outfield pavilion.

9.5 Perspective view of Blue Street, a new ground-level outfield concourse with elevated pathways and a variety of year-round retailers.

9.4

9.5

9.6

9.6 View within the proposed Hall of Fame museum behind the Batter's Eye; A/R and V/R components allow fans to browse through the Dodgers' history and even interact with events on the field in real time.

9.7

9.7 Postcard shot from the top deck, looking toward the centerfield additions.

9.8 Plan and section through the proposed Blue Street addition behind and underneath the existing outfield pavilions.

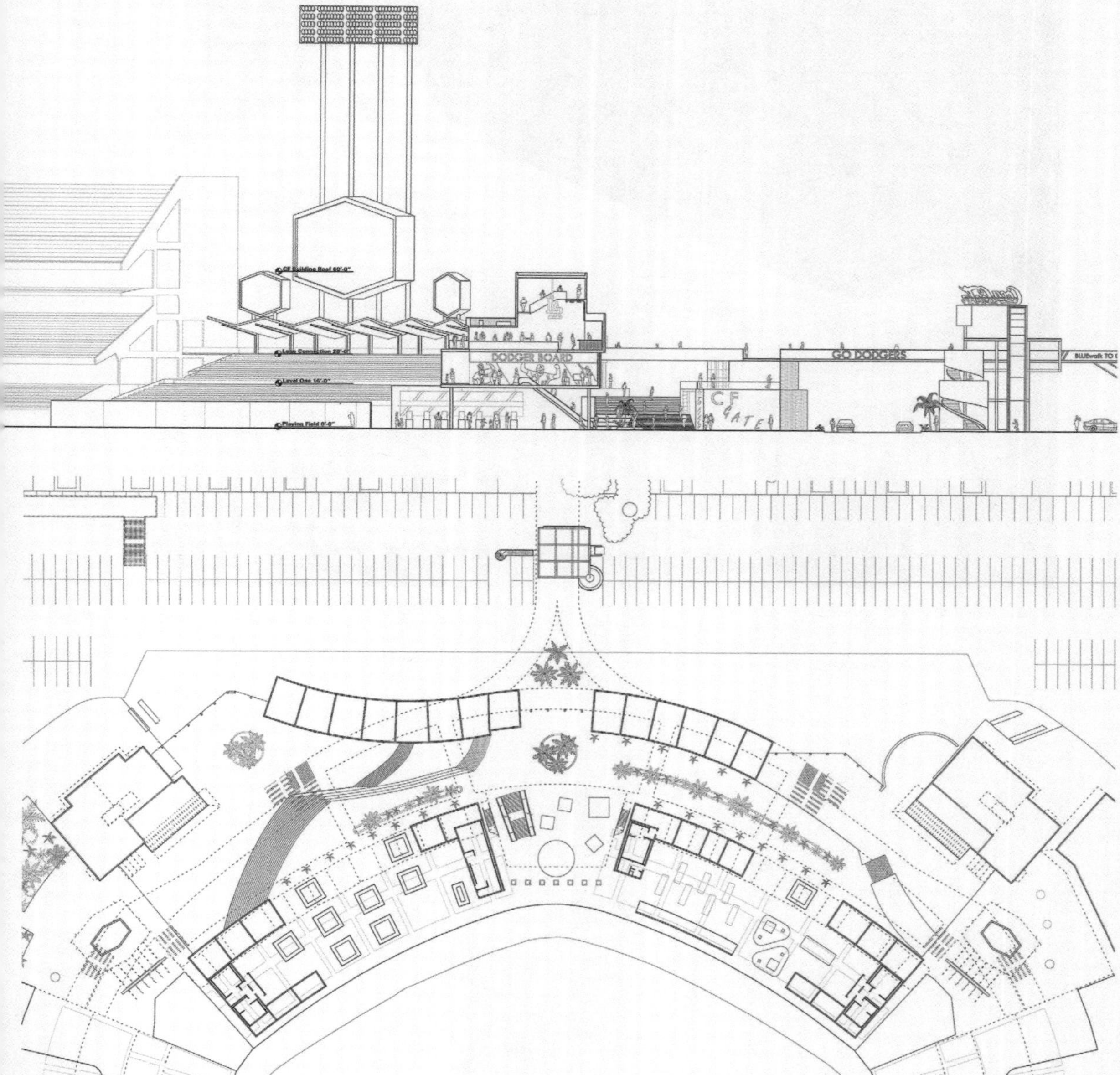
CF Building Roof 60'-0"
Loge Connection 28'-0"
Level One 16'-0"
Playing Field 0'-0"
DODGER BOARD
GO DODGERS
BLUEwalk TO
CF GATE

9.8

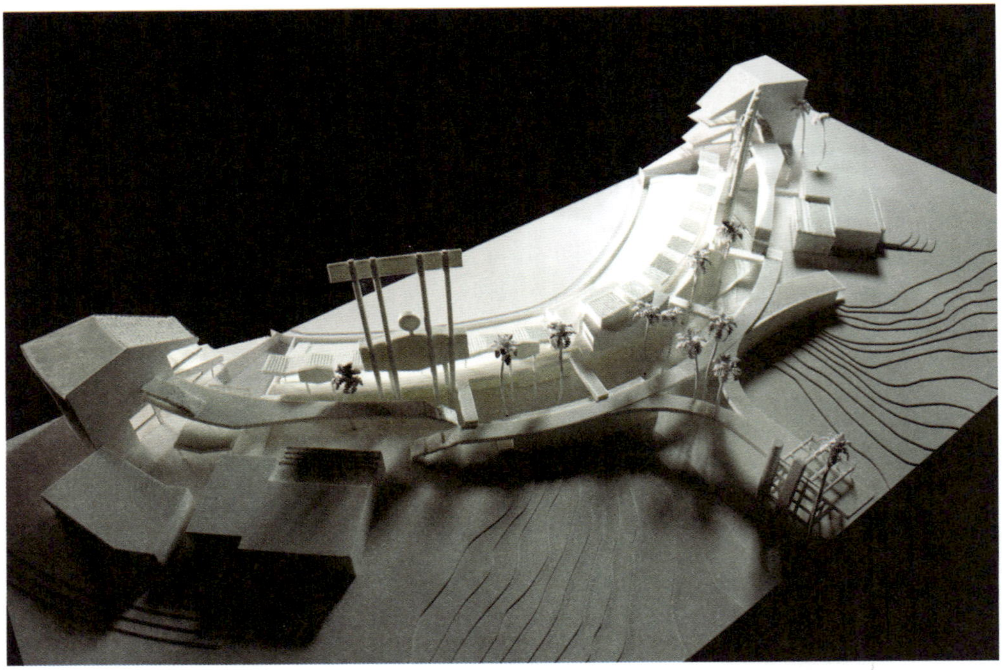

9.9

9.9 Southwest-facing view of model.

9.10 East-facing view of model.

9.10

Extras

A Discussion with Larry Lucchino and Stan Kasten

Ron Ostezan What is a successful ballpark today? For those with a strong history, is capturing the nostalgia of the place an important step? For new ballparks, is creating a "unique" experience important?

Stan Kasten Not every city has as much equity in its history as Los Angeles, Boston, Chicago, or New York City, and I think it is always a mistake to try to manufacture that. Most baseball fans want a variety of amenities, a variety of views, a variety of concessions; more and more, modern customers aren't used to just sitting in their seats for nine innings. They want to have other opportunities, which is what the twenty-first century is about. We try to provide for both.

RO How do you decide whether to renovate an existing facility or move to another site? Given Major League Baseball's difficulty in attracting younger fans, are new methods of viewership and ballpark activities necessary when thinking about projects for the future?

Larry Lucchino We certainly look forward when designing for current or future realities. First, you have to recognize that not every team or market or city is the same. They are not fungible; they are not interchangeable. Something that is right in one place may not be right in another. A ballpark might be the right thing to do in Baltimore, a renovation might be the right thing to do in Boston—you can't apply a one-size-fits-all approach. You have to be careful about the condition of the existing facility: is it decrepit or is it just run down with very strong bones and could therefore be renovated? Should it be renovated? I think you need to consider the marketplace, the quality of the facility, and the alternative models you can develop there. Whatever you do, it depends on the individual ballpark, the particular vision, the particular city, and whatever urban planning needs there may be. It's a combination of factors that needs to be considered, but one size does not fit all.

RO Are there ways to attract both the die-hard fan and the spectator who is just coming for the experience?

SK The 1950s was the so-called golden age of baseball; it was a great time for a team to draw a million fans because a million fans paid the bills. A million fans do not pay the bills anymore. Today, you need two million fans, maybe two and a half million fans or three million fans. And I can't get three million fans purely on hard-core baseball—I need to reach out to men, to women, to kids, to seniors and to new fans as well as old fans. I need to do things to attract and engage the entire spectrum of fans. For modern fans, the obvious things are the best scoreboards, the best Wi-Fi, the best sound system, and the best entertainment. Baseball has an advantage: Unlike continuous-action sports—such as hockey and basketball, where you don't really have a chance to look away from what is going on—baseball games have three hundred breaks in the action every night, and that is the ten to twenty seconds in between each pitch. That is the next horizon for us. How do we program breaks in the action in exciting, engaging,

appealing ways? I don't know if the answer is highlights, gambling propositions, texting, video, statistics, or games the fans can play—for example, interactions with other people in the stands. I don't know what it is exactly, I don't know the right mix, and the formula for it could be different from city to city. But that is the real opportunity: programming the lulls in the action that brings fans into our sport.

RO With more and more ballparks accommodating outside events (concerts, other sports, and so on), do you see the need for flexible venues?

SK Baseball is different from sports that play on a rectangle—football, basketball, hockey. Setting the concept in a stadium is just cooler and more fun than staying in another rectangular box building. I think a unique, distinctive baseball stadium will always have an extra element of cool. How important is it to have outside events? All the revenue we get is important for getting our jobs done, but it is

Students and instructors behind home plate during batting practice at Petco Park.

a small part of our business. I can't say it is an overwhelmingly important thing, but it helps, and we have an advantage at Dodger Stadium in that we are a fundamentally distinctive venue—that always is appealing.

RO Dodger Stadium, Fenway Park, and other iconic venues have survived when many others have not. What can venues do to ensure their future existence?

SK Now, structurally, I don't think there is a reason the Dodgers can't operate here indefinitely. I don't mean like the Colosseum in Rome, but we see no end date in sight. Let's face it, there are already some other stadiums in baseball that have been in operation for more than a hundred years, and this stadium can do that and beyond. The first thing that had to be done when we got here was wiring and plumbing, and we did that. We brought in modern things—for example, we installed the largest Wi-Fi system in baseball. Dodger Stadium is the safest ballpark in baseball.

RO Given the reluctance of cities today to provide public funding for entertainment facilities such as sports; how do teams convince cities to acquire the funding necessary to complete such projects?

LL I would take issue with the phrasing of the question—"entertainment facilities." Ballparks can be much more than that. They can be community-gathering places, and they can be economic catalysts for downtown redevelopment—they can play a lot of roles. I think I have seen the evolution in public-private financing plans. Many years ago, they were exclusively public: the city was the landlord, and we were the tenant. Now, there has been an evolution, and it has changed a good bit. But there are still public interests and private interests. And because there are both, there should be some kind of financing plan that accommodates civic interests, private interests, and sport interests.

RO When did this shift happen? Has it been a recent change or has it been a long time coming?

LL It is shifting over time. When we did Camden Yards in Baltimore with Janet Marie Smith, the pendulum was on the other side. It was almost exclusively public funding, and we were paying a fair rent. That has changed over time and now includes the involvement of the private sector. There is both public and private benefit in the project. It can be an important urban planning device; it can be an important urban revitalization catalyst. In the cities where I have been involved—Baltimore, San Diego, Boston, and now Worcester—there are demonstrable public benefits and private benefits. Therefore, the financing is in both.

RO Larry, you have worked on three Major League Baseball stadiums—for the Baltimore Orioles, the San Diego Padres, and the Boston Red Sox. What are some interesting opportunities in your project for the Pawtucket Red Sox minor-league team?

LL There are 160 affiliated minor-league teams, so that is 160 small cities and towns in America that could benefit from a strategic development of a ballpark. I think the opportunities for impact are particularly great within the minor leagues. Secondly, the product is different. Major League Baseball is about baseball; Minor League Baseball is about affordable family entertainment. Minor-league baseball parks are oftentimes within the reach of small towns because the capacity is limited. They are not parks with a 40,000 or 50,000 capacity; the capacity might be 5,000 to 10,000. Consequently, there is more opportunity to use these vehicles in smaller towns across America.

RO Perhaps one of the biggest challenges with Dodger Stadium is the transportation to and from the stadium. Stan, how important is it to consider the larger scale to connect a sports venue to the city?

SK We are always studying traffic patterns in Los Angeles and doing things to make it as efficient as we can for 50,000 people in a confined area. We are also looking for newer alternatives—such as the gondola from Union Station downtown or the Boring Company's experiment [an underground tunnel for high-speed transportation]—to help bring people here faster. We will never be able to move Dodger Stadium, and we are not downtown. For some customers, that is a fundamental challenge. On the other hand, it is important that I remind people that, for more than fifty years, 50,000 people have found their way here annually. And if it were as big a problem as many in the media make it seem, then that would not be the case. So, yes, we need to keep working on making it easier and more convenient, but let's give the fans credit for their ability to get here, even under the current conditions.

RO Would you like to say a few words on the studio?

LL I was very impressed by the work that the Yale architectural graduate students did in exploring several different New England cities and what kind of ballparks they sensed in those particular cities. I think the thoughtfulness and labor that they put into it was exceptional. There was some substantive creative work that went into each of the projects. And I feel that we owe Janet Marie Smith and the Yale School of Architecture a lot of gratitude.

SK I enjoyed the entire project. I was thrilled Janet was able to spend time at Yale. There is not a better person in the world to have participated. I think the students all came up with innovative ideas. I can't point to one thing that was incorporated and one thing that wasn't, but it all involved some really good thinking for our team when we got into it, and we are still in the process of designing what the final product will be. But all of it was very valuable to the Dodgers, and we are thrilled that we were able to participate.

Students with Janet Marie Smith following midterm reviews.

Continued Student Work With the Pawtucket RedSox

The work of the students was fruitful after the studio ended. In fact, when the PawSox were negotiating with Pawtucket and Worcester, management asked two student teams to present their projects. (The current lease of McCoy Stadium, home of the PawSox, ends in 2020.)

In November 2017, the Worcester team (Justin Lai and Jiajian Min) presented to city officials with Larry Lucchino and Janet Marie Smith. They presented to Edward M. Augustus Jr., Worcester's city manager, as well as state of Massachusetts officials and a local developer with a project for the site. Talks focused on

From left to right, Dylan Weiser, Valeria Flores, and Zach Hoffmann present their project to the city of Pawtucket.

the opportunities for the revitalization of the Canal District through the creation of an urban ballpark. City officials and local developers were enthusiastic about the team's presentation.

Alongside Larry Lucchino, Janet Marie Smith, and Alan Plattus, the Pawtucket team of the Slater Mills site (Valeria Flores, Zachary Hoffmann, and Dylan Weiser) presented to Pawtucket officials, including the mayor, and numerous residents. The proposal's riverfront development acted as a catalyst for new development in the city, working in conjunction with the city's new train station. While some were concerned with the project's cost and potential to generate noise in residential areas, the design was generally well received due to its integration with the historic downtown, its potential to revitalize the city and sprout new development, and its prospect to retain the hometown team.

After months of deliberations, the PawSox have announced the team is moving to Worcester in 2021.

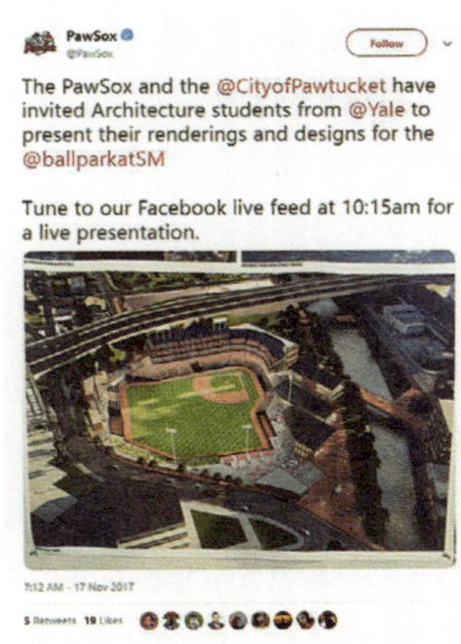
PawSox
Follow
The PawSox and the @CityofPawtucket have invited Architecture students from @Yale to present their renderings and designs for the @ballparkatSM

Tune to our Facebook live feed at 10:15am for a live presentation.

7:12 AM - 17 Nov 2017

Biographies

Janet Marie Smith

Janet Marie Smith has been the Los Angeles Dodgers' senior vice president of planning and development since 2012, overseeing $200 million in construction renovations. Called the "Ballpark Whisperer" by *Sports Illustrated* author Steve Rushin, Smith is best known for her work on the influential Oriole Park at Camden Yards in Baltimore, leading the effort as vice president of planning and development for that organization.

Smith previously was president of Turner Sports and Entertainment Development, a division of Turner Broadcasting System, and was the vice president of planning and development for the Atlanta Braves. Her work in Atlanta helped to transform the 1996 Olympic Stadium into Turner Field and she oversaw the development of the Philips Arena, home of the National Basketball Association's Atlanta Hawks and the National Hockey League's Atlanta Thrashers. She served as senior vice president of planning and development for the Boston Red Sox from 2002–09, overseeing the preservation of historic Fenway Park in Boston and leading the program that placed the ballpark on the National Historic Register.

In 2017, *Sports Business Journal* named Smith a "Champion: Pioneer & Innovator in Sports Business." In 2014, she was a recipient of a Women of Inspiration Award from the Los Angeles chapter of Women in Sports & Events (WISE). In 2012, the Boston Baseball Writers honored Smith with a special achievement award for her work at Fenway Park. In 2011, she was included in the inaugural class of the *Sports Business Journal's* "Game Changers: Women in Sports

Business." She has been active with the Urban Land Institute, the American Institute of Architects, and the American Planning Association. She serves on the advisory board for the University of Michigan's sports management program.

Andrei Harwell

Andrei Harwell is an architect, urban designer, and design educator with twenty years of experience developing award-winning projects that respond to contemporary challenges that confront U.S. and global cities, towns, and urban regions. Harwell has designed buildings, parks, and public spaces and produced neighborhood, downtown, and regional plans for a range of clients. He is currently design director of the Yale Urban Design Workshop, where he has authored plans for Connecticut's Thames River Heritage Park, for Fishers Island, New York, and coordinated the urban design of a major HUD-funded resilience project in Bridgeport, Connecticut. A critic in architecture at the Yale School of Architecture since 2007, he has taught numerous advanced studios and a summer traveling seminar, in Gothenburg, Sweden. He holds a BArch from Carnegie Mellon University and a MArch from Yale.

Alan J. Plattus

Alan J. Plattus is professor of architecture and urbanism at the Yale School of Architecture, where he teaches courses on architectural history and theory as well as urban history and design; also, he directed the school's China Studio for fifteen years. He is visiting professor at Chalmers University, in Gothenburg, Sweden, where he consults on the city's Fusion Point project. He founded and directs the Yale Urban Design Workshop (YUDW), a community design center that has undertaken urban design and building projects throughout Connecticut, including recent HUD-funded coastal resilience planning in Bridgeport, and, as part of an international team, the design of the Peace Park on the Israel-Jordan border. He has lectured and published on the history of cities, civic pageantry, modern architecture, and urbanism and served on the boards of the Association of Collegiate Schools of Architecture, the National Architecture Accrediting Board, the Connecticut Main Street Center, the Eli Whitney Museum, and the *Journal of Architectural Education*. He has a BA from Yale University and an MArch from Princeton University. He is part of a family of fairly rabid Boston Red Sox fans.

Studio Participants

Heewon Choi
Daniel Fetcho
Valeria Flores
Zachary Hoffmann
Justin Lai
Audrey Yifei Li
Jiajian Min
Ron Ostezan
Christine Tran
Dylan Weiser

Image Credits

Andrei Harwell 18, 22, 24, 26, 31, 33, 34, 43, 44, 47, 49, 53, 105
Audrey Yifei Li 40, 84–91, 122–128
Christine Tran 41, 43, 53, 84–91, 122–128, 143, 145
Daniel Fetcho 38, 66-73, 130–139
Dylan Weiser 34, 40, 75–82, 12–120
Heewon Choi 41, 84–91, 122–128, 130–139
Janet Marie Smith 17, 21, 22
Justin Lai 38, 93–101, 130–139
Min Jiajian 37, 93–101
Ron Ostezan 39, 66–73, 130–139
Valeria Flores 37, 75–82, 112–120
Zachary Hoffmann 39, 75–82, 112–120

Note: Some images of student projects have advertisements to suggest potential sponsorship opportunities or to accurately portray visual situations at ballparks today. These are included in this book as representations of student work. In no way does the Yale School of Architecture endorse these advertisements.